D0889898

HERO

On a

MISSION

HERO

On a

MISSION

· · · · · · · · · · · · · · · · · · · ·

A Path to a Meaningful Life

DONALD MILLER

HarperCollins
Leadership

An Imprint of HarperCollins

Published by HarperCollins Leadership, an imprint of HarperCollins Focus LLC.

Any internet addresses, phone numbers, or company or product information printed in this book are offered as a resource and are not intended in any way to be or to imply an endorsement by HarperCollins Leadership, nor does HarperCollins Leadership vouch for the existence, content, or services of these sites, phone numbers, companies, or products beyond the life of this book.

ISBN 978-1-4002-2802-7 (eBook)
ISBN 978-1-4002-2694-8 (HC)

Library of Congress Cataloging-in-Publication Data
Library of Congress Cataloging-in-Publication application has been submitted.

Printed in the United States of America
22 23 24 25 26 LSC 10 9 8 7 6 5 4 3 2 1

For Emmeline Miller

This book comes with a free Hero on a Mission Life Plan and Daily Planner. Scan the QR code below to download your life plan and daily planner pages:

Table of Contents

. . . .

Act 1
How to Create a Life of Meaning

Act 2
Create Your Life Plan

Act 3
Your Life Plan and Daily Planner

. . . .

Author's Note

. . . .

I don't think any of us should trust fate to write the story of our lives.

Fate is a terrible writer.

Introduction

In stories, there are four primary characters:

1. The victim is the character who feels they have no way out.
2. The villain is the character who makes others small.
3. The hero is the character who faces their challenges and transforms.
4. The guide is the character who helps the hero.

As you read a story or watch a movie, you feel sympathy for the victim, you cheer for the hero, you hate the villain, and you respect the guide.

These four characters exist in stories not only because they exist in the real world, but because they exist inside you and me.

In my life I play all four characters every day. If I'm faced with an unfair challenge, I usually play the victim for a minute, feeling sorry for myself. If I am wronged, I dream about vengeance, like a villain. If I come up with a good idea and want to make it happen, I switch into hero mode to take action, and if somebody calls and needs my advice, I play the guide.

The problem is these characters are not equal. Two help us experience a deep sense of meaning and two lead to our demise.

For many years I mostly played the victim, and this mindset negatively affected the quality of my life. As I'll explain in the book, I did not like myself. I did not like my life and was not respected by others. I also didn't make any money, did not have healthy relationships, and was not competent as a professional.

My life played out like a sad tragedy, and it would have gone on that way if I'd not discovered something.

I realized that my problem was not my circumstances or my upbringing or even past trauma; my problem was the way I viewed myself. Again, I viewed myself as a victim.

As I understood more about the powerful characteristics of heroes in literature and in movies, though, I became curious about whether embodying some of those characteristics would create a better life experience.

Living like a hero (which is nothing like you might think—heroes are anything but strong and capable; they are simply victims going through a process of transformation) entered me into, unknowingly, something called logotherapy, a therapy created by a Viennese psychologist named Viktor Frankl. I will explain much more about logotherapy in this book.

Entering into logotherapy changed my life for the better. I went from being sad to being content. I went from unproductive to productive. And I went from having certain fears of close relationships to being able to enter into and enjoy those relationships. Mostly, though, I went from feeling life was meaningless to experiencing a deep sense of meaning.

About ten years into living this way, I created a life plan and daily planner that helped me turn all of these helpful ideas into a system. And that's what this book is about. It's about living like a hero so you can experience a deep sense of meaning. The book teaches a simple-to-use system allowing anybody to live a life that delivers a deep sense of meaning.

If you have struggled with a feeling of futility, or if you are tired of the story you've been living, or if you are having to start over and create a new reality for yourself, I hope you find this book to be helpful.

ACT

1

How to Create a Life of Meaning

1

. . . .

The Victim, the Villain, the Hero, and the Guide: The Four Roles We Play in Life

LIVING A MEANING-FILLED STORY does not happen by accident. In fact, living a good story is a lot like writing one. When we read a great story, we don't realize the hours of daydreaming, planning, fits, and false starts that went into what the reader may experience as a clean line of meaningful action.

Stories can be fun to write and fun to live, but the good ones take work.

Whether we like it or not, the lives we live are stories. Our lives have a beginning, middle, and end, and inside those three acts we play many roles. We are brothers and sisters, sons and daughters, mothers and fathers, teammates, lovers, friends, and so much more. For many of us, the stories we live feel meaningful, interesting, and perhaps even inspired. For others, life feels as though the writer has lost the plot.

All of this begs the question, though: Who is writing our stories? Is God writing our stories? Is fate writing our stories? Is the government or our boss or the church writing our stories? I heard an interview with a physicist who espoused the possibility our stories actually don't exist in time at all and that they have not yet started and are already done at the same time, or rather in the absence of time. Perhaps this is true but even if it is, I'm not sure how it helps me enjoy life any more or less. The truth is, we all have to live this life and experience it within the confines of time and I'm guessing we all want the experience to be as meaningful as possible.

For practical purposes, it is my position that the author of our stories is actually us. Perhaps the single greatest paradigm shift I've had as a human is this idea: I am writing my story and I alone have the responsibility to shape it into something meaningful.

I agree with James Allen, who said in his 1902 book *As a Man Thinketh*, "Man is buffeted by circumstances so long as he believes himself to be the creature of outside conditions, but when he realizes that he is a creative power, and that he may command the hidden soil and seeds of his being out of which circumstances grow, he then becomes the rightful master of himself."

Here is a hard truth: if God is writing our stories, He isn't doing a good job. I think we can all agree that some people's stories seem quite tragic and many of us have experienced our share of those tragedies. What's more, if God is writing our stories, He isn't doing a fair job either. Some people are born privileged, and some are not. Some people die an untimely death, and others live in prime health until their credits roll.

What if, instead of writing our stories, God has invented the sunrise and sunset, the ocean and the desert, love and various forms of weather and then handed us the pen to write the proverbial rest?

What if we are much more responsible for the quality of our stories than we previously thought? What if any restlessness we feel about our lives is not in fact the fault of fate, but the fault of the writer themselves and that writer is us?

What if the broken nature of life is a fact, but the idea we can also create something meaningful in the midst of that brokenness is an equal fact?

None of this can be proven, of course, but does it need to be proven to be a useful paradigm?

Also, if I believe fate has all the power and so I sit neutral as my story wanders aimlessly around the page like it was dictated by a dispassionate imbecile, who should I blame? God? Fate? Steinbeck?

It seems to me that blaming myself is the most viable option. While that option may implicate me, it also offers me the most power to do something about it.

Regardless of who is writing our stories, it is a useful belief that we are the authors. And it's more than a useful belief: it's a fun belief. What if we get to partner with the fixed elements of life to carve out a little narrative of our own making?

If we are tired of life, what we're really tired of is the story we are living inside of. And the great thing about being tired of our story is that stories can be edited. Stories can be fixed. Stories can go from dull to exciting, from rambling to focused, and from drudgery to read to exhilarating to live.

All we need to know to fix our stories are the principles that make a story meaningful. Then, if we apply those principles to our lives and stop handing our pen to fate, we can change our personal experience and in turn feel gratitude for its beauty, rather than resentment for its meaninglessness.

THE VICTIM: THE ONE WHO FEELS LIKE THEY HAVE NO WAY OUT

If you were a writer and came to me with a troubled story and said, "Don, this story isn't working. It's not interesting and I don't know how to fix it," the first thing I'd look at is the lead character. Who is this story about and why isn't this character working to make the story meaningful?

As I mentioned in the introduction, there are four major characters in nearly every story: the victim, the villain, the hero, and the guide. One thing that will ruin a story fast is if the hero—the character that the story is about—acts like a victim.

You cannot have a lead character in a story that acts like a victim. This is true in stories and it's true in life. In fact, this is true in stories *because* it's true in life.

The reason a hero that acts like a victim ruins the story is because a story must move forward to be interesting. The hero must want something that is difficult and perhaps even frightening to achieve. This is the plot of nearly every inspirational story you've ever read.

A victim, on the other hand, does not move forward or accept challenges. Instead, a victim gives up because they have come to believe they are doomed.

If you think about it, then, a person who surrenders their life to fate is the essence of a victim. By surrendering their story to fate, they allow fate to decide whether they succeed in a career, experience intimacy, cultivate a sense of gratitude, or set an example for their children. Fate, then, does a terrific job managing the scenery but little to push the plot of the hero forward. That job was the hero's to do and they didn't do it.

Likely we all know a person or two who seems to live this way. Or worse, we may actually live this way ourselves!

Victims believe they are helpless and so flail until they are rescued.

Actual victims do exist and do in fact need to be rescued. Victimhood, however, is a temporary state. Once rescued, the better story is that we return to the heroic energy that moves our story forward.

The truth is, I used to be gloomy and sad myself. When I was in my midtwenties, I hit a stall. I rented a small room in a house in Portland, Oregon, and slept on a low-slung couch-bed that folded out to form a lumpy mattress on the floor. I'd wake in the morning and stare at the carpet just beyond my nose, wondering at the specks of cereal in the fibers.

It was more than twenty years ago. I lived in a house with a group of guys who were likely unimpressed with my lack of ambition and uninspired by my lack of action.

I'd handed my pen to fate and fate seemed to have been on a bender or perhaps distracted by the extra attention it was giving to the story of Justin Timberlake. (If fate does write our stories, and I cannot prove that it doesn't, it did a terrific job with Justin Timberlake's.) Regardless, the lack of plan wasn't working. I was terribly unhealthy and sad and going nowhere. I believed life was hard and that fate was working against me.

Getting off a soft mattress on the floor isn't as easy as getting out of a bed, so in the morning I'd lie there an extra hour, wondering if we had a vacuum cleaner. Then, I'd roll over onto my knees and push myself up with what were supposed to be arms. I wondered every morning if I had arthritis. I was twenty-six.

Because I surfaced so much victim energy, my career went nowhere. I knew I wanted to be a writer but I wasn't doing anything about it. My story bogged down in inaction. I had yet to write a book or even try. I wanted to write, for sure, but in my victim energy I believed writing books was for people who were smarter than me or more disciplined or for people who spoke with a British accent. I did not believe I could actually become somebody who wrote books because fate determined who could write books and fate did not particularly like me. After all, fate had not given me a British accent.

Back when I was surfacing mostly victim energy, I remember riding a bus downtown to sell a few books to the used book buyers at Powell's. Powell's is a big bookstore in downtown Portland that will buy your library for about a third of what they can resell it for. I often sold my books so I could afford a slice of pizza. I remember riding the bus back home and seeing the line of homeless people outside the rescue mission. I was three days from having to pay rent that I didn't have. I remember being afraid I'd be in that line the following week.

I didn't know it at the time, but what I needed more than anything was a belief that I was actually the one writing my story, and then some kind of structure to help me live a story that would produce a sense of meaning. I needed to know my story could be edited and changed, and I needed principles I could use in the process.

Many of us likely identify with that season. We've all been through periods of hopelessness. Some make it out and others stay in the hopeless state. Most of us, though, choose a hybrid life. We move forward a little, maybe get a career and a spouse and some kids, but we continue to be halted by intrusions of victim energy. We only surface hero energy when we need to climb a rung in our career or clean ourselves up so we can find a mate and reproduce. But to the degree victim energy surfaces in our lives, our stories suffer a haunting restlessness.

Again, if a story is going to work, the hero must not surface victim energy. Victim energy is a belief that we are helpless, that we are doomed.

The point is this: even before we ask ourselves what our story is about, we have to ask ourselves what character we are playing within that story. If we are playing the victim or the villain, no amount of editing can help us. In the story of life, we will have played a bit part and our story will fail to gain narrative traction.

Be careful, though. If by reading these words we realize we've been surfacing victim energy and shame ourselves, we've immediately surfaced another kind of energy that will ruin our story. We've surfaced villain energy. A villain, you see, makes others small. A story about a villain won't deliver a sense of meaning either.

When we shame ourselves for acting like a victim, we're manifesting a conversation in which the villain inside us attacks the victim inside us. This kind of inner dialogue does not create a great story either.

In fact, the two characters that will ruin our story the fastest are the victim and the villain.

THE VILLAIN: THE ONE WHO MAKES OTHERS SMALL

The second item on our checklist for fixing a bad story is to make sure the hero isn't surfacing too much villain energy. Just like a hero that surfaces victim energy, a hero that surfaces villain energy will ruin the story too.

I don't take for granted you're going to stick with me just because you paid money for this book. I'll warn you now: if you don't like characters who feel jealous of others and belittle their lives and accomplishments, you're not going to like me either because I did all those things.

Back before I learned how to edit my story, I defaulted to villain energy all the time.

Because I was sad about my sad life and jealous of people passing me by, I made other people small.

Specifically, the guys I lived with had lives that were moving forward, which made the fact mine was standing still feel all the worse. They were dating girls they'd later marry. They were starting jobs that would become careers. They were developing rhythms in life that would lead to success. I, on the other hand, was unable to find a beat.

So I took it out on them.

Mostly I was passive-aggressive. I'd make negative comments about the things they loved.

"Watching soccer on television is a little like watching fish in an aquarium, don't you think?"

One time they made a rule that nobody could leave their dishes in the sink. They made that rule mostly because I left dishes in the sink. One morning when I woke up and the house was empty, I saw that the guys hadn't cleaned up after breakfast, so I put the dirty dishes in their beds. Note that the other guys had beds.

As I've already said, villains try to make other people small. Looking back, that's what I was doing. I felt so small that I needed other people to be smaller so I could feel big. I needed their girlfriends to be uninteresting and their jobs to be a joke.

Don't hate on the villain too badly though. The truth is they've had a rough go of it. In stories, heroes and villains have a similar backstory. They start out as victims. Pay attention the next time you watch a movie or read a book. Surprisingly often, the hero begins as an orphan. The story begins with them losing a parent or having to live with their hairy uncle. Then they are rejected and bullied at school. The other kids shove trash into their backpacks and put their books in the toilet.

The villain is no different. There is pain for them too.

The story doesn't usually tell the backstory of the villain, but the writers almost always allude to some kind of torment in the character's past. That's why the villain has a scar across their face, or a limp, or a speech impediment. The storyteller wants you to know the villain is carrying a pain they've not dealt with.

What separates a villain from a hero is the hero learns from their pain and tries to help others avoid the same pain. The villain, on the other hand, seeks vengeance against the world that hurt them.

The difference between the villain and the hero is the way they react to the pain they've experienced.

In stories, villain energy brings about negative consequences. The more we surface that energy, the worse our stories get.

This is all light treatment when it comes to villains. The truth is, the energies we each surface exist on a spectrum. If we learn the coping mechanisms of a villain and reinforce those mechanisms over time, we can become diabolical. Many people have. In their book *Personality Types*, Don Richard Riso and Russ Hudson chart the negative decline of each of nine personality types. Some of the personality types, when in descent, will eventually abuse those weaker than them as a way of feeling secure in their power. The other types are hardly better, each of us getting worse as we decline and all of us ending up in prison, or committing murder or suicide.

Our villainous tendencies may seem innocent enough, but villain energy is nothing to take lightly. When we begin to reduce others in our minds, we are dancing with the devil.

When I operated out of villain energy, I became more and more isolated. My roommates didn't want to sit and talk. Girls whizzed by my bedroom door to visit the other guys without stopping to say hello. Who wants to sit and talk to a person who is brooding and resentful?

My villain energy caused my roommates to stage an intervention to talk about how difficult I'd become. It was a tough season, but ultimately I had to admit to myself they were right. My story was going nowhere because my character was wrapped up in victim and villain coping mechanisms, rather than accepting the challenge of life itself and stepping into my challenges with courage.

We know we are surfacing villain energy when we dismiss other people's comments or when we think of them as lesser. We know we are surfacing villain energy when we reduce others to their outward appearances rather than taking the time to understand their point of view. We know we are surfacing villain energy when we reduce those who criticize us rather than seek to learn and grow. If we are honest, we all surface villain energy all the time, sometimes depending on whether or not we've skipped lunch.

Another reason not to play the villain is that, like victims, villains do not experience a transformation. Villains are the same bitter menace at the end of the story as they are at the beginning. Not only this, but villains, like victims, play a bit part in the story. For all their power and might and bluster, villains are only in a story to make the hero look good and elicit sympathy for the victim. For as much attention as the villain gets, the story isn't about them.

THE HERO: THE ONE WILLING TO FACE THEIR CHALLENGES AND TRANSFORM

What I learned over time, and what this book is about, is that playing the hero improves our stories dramatically. If we want to take control of our lives and bend our story toward meaning, we can surface more hero energy and less victim and villain energy.

I am grateful for this revelation because it likely saved my life and certainly saved the quality of my life.

What is the essence of heroic energy? A hero wants something in life and is willing to accept challenges in order to transform into the person capable of getting what they want.

When we're reading a story or watching a movie, we subconsciously want the hero to rise to the occasion.

This is one of the questions I would certainly ask myself as I edited a story that wasn't working. How is the hero responding to their challenge? When they are insulted, how do they react? When they are rejected, how do they treat the person who has rejected them? When they feel that all is lost, are they able to find a light in the darkness? Do they try? Do they move forward against all odds, and do they get up again when they are knocked down?

If the hero responds with purposeful action and a sense of hope, our story will move forward and become interesting. But if they respond with a sense of hopelessness like a victim, or if they lash out at others like a villain, the story will break down.

THE CHARACTER WE PLAY WILL DETERMINE THE QUALITY OF OUR STORY

What we're really talking about when we talk about what character we play in the story of our lives is identity. Who do we believe we are? If we believe we are helpless and our stories are in the hands of fate, we are operating from a victim identity. If we believe other people are small and should do as we say, we are operating from a villain identity.

The first shift we experience as we surface heroic energy, though, is that our lives are not in the hands of fate. At least not completely. Heroes rise up with courage to change their circumstances.

Fate may send us challenges, but it does not dictate how we respond to those challenges. We are not preprogrammed. We have the power to shape our own stories. Fate may throw us sunshine or rain, but it does not determine who we are. We determine who we are, and who we are directs our story more than anything or anybody else.

When we look at a perfectly capable person who sadly sees themselves as a victim, there's a temptation to judge them for not having discipline. But discipline isn't their problem. Their problem is in their identity. They do not know they have heroic energy within them.

The more I learned the principles that help create a good story and the more I applied them to my life, the more I transformed how I viewed myself and the more meaningful my life experience became.

Identity, in fact, is how the good parts of my story began. The journey began with curiosity about who I could become.

I'd been buying and selling books at Powell's for the better part of two years. Whenever I got money, I'd buy books, and whenever I ran out I'd sell them back. It was a losing game, of course, but man does not live by pizza alone. I loved the words and I wanted to write them myself. I started to get more and more curious, and even a little hopeful, about whether I could actually become a writer.

Transformation didn't happen immediately. I continued to vacillate between victim, villain, and hero energy depending on the day and sometimes even the hour. But slowly, over time, I began to play the hero more and the victim and villain less, and that made all the difference.

Nearly every day, I would write. And nearly every day I wrote got a little better.

Transforming from victim mindset to hero mindset started with a question: *Who could I become?* Just knowing there was a possibility I could become a writer, that I could accomplish something meaningful, gave me the courage to take a risk and try.

Every inspiring person I know started with a similar curiosity about who they could become or what they could create. Think of the people who have inspired you. One day they picked up a guitar, or plugged a transistor into a computer, or narrowed the nozzle on the bottom of a rocket engine, and thirty years later they had changed the world.

I'll spend the rest of this book unpacking the characteristics of a hero. We'd be confused, however, if we said any of us succeeded at the hero's journey on our own. Heroes have help. Lots of help. There are people in our lives who show us a better way to live.

A hero gets help from a guide.

THE GUIDE: THE ONE WHO HELPS THE HERO

If I were trying to fix a broken story, after I made sure the hero wasn't manifesting too much victim or villain energy, the next thing I'd look for is the guide. Who is helping the hero win? Where is the hero getting their knowledge from? Who is the hero going to for encouragement?

In stories, heroes can't make it on their own because they don't know how. If they knew how, they would have worked out all those flaws on their own.

Remember, heroes are flawed and in need of transformation. In fact, they are often the second weakest character in a story. Only the victim is in worse shape.

To help the hero out, the storyteller sends a guide. Yoda helped Luke learn to be a Jedi. Haymitch helped Katniss win the Hunger Games.

Much of the help I needed to become a writer came from those books I read at Powell's. John Steinbeck's *Journal of a Novel* taught me the discipline and joy of writing. *A Moveable Feast* by Ernest Hemingway taught me how to pace a book. Annie Dillard's *An American Childhood* taught me to make the writing visual. Anne Lamott's *Traveling Mercies* taught me honesty was akin to courage.

Guides are the characters in the story who have empathy and confidence, and as such are equipped to help the hero win.

The confidence guides have comes from their years of experience honing in their own hero's journey. Guides know what they are doing and can pass valuable knowledge on to the hero.

The empathy guides have comes from their pain. As you've likely guessed, guides have backstories of pain too.

Like victims, villains, and heroes, guides have had to overcome challenges, injustices, and even tragedies. Think of Nelson Mandela in his jail cell on Robben Island, or Helen Keller learning to write and speak though she could not see or hear words.

Pain, then, is often the teacher that transforms the hero into the guide. That is, if their attitude toward pain is accepting and redemptive.

The main characteristic of a guide is that they help the hero win. That help must come from experience, and the most important experience they have to have had is in turning difficult situations into opportunities to transform.

When you watch a story, the story itself is not about the guide; it's about the hero, and yet the guide is the strongest, most capable character in the story. They are also the most caring and compassionate. We may root for the hero and hate the villain, but our utmost respect is reserved for the guide.

When you think of guides in stories, think of Mr. Miyagi in *The Karate Kid* or Lionel in *The King's Speech*. Think of Mary Poppins, guiding the family into a new and better understanding of life itself.

To me, becoming a guide is the most meaningful transformation that can happen in a human life.

Even as I write these words, my wife, Betsy, is pregnant with our first child. Nothing has caused me more curiosity about the characteristics of a guide than the knowledge we are about to become parents.

We do not live this life to build a monument to ourselves, but to pass our understanding of life on to those who come behind us so that their stories can be even more meaningful than ours.

What if the story of our lives is less about what we build and more about who we build up?

How much more meaningful would our stories be if, at our funeral, people talked less about our accomplishments and more about our encouragement?

If life is teaching us anything, it seems to be this: it is a meaningful thing to sacrifice ourselves for the sake of another. This is the essence of a guide, and if we take the hero's journey, this is where each of our stories will go.

TO LIVE A STORY IS NOT A CHOICE

The hard truth about life is not that it asks us to live a story, but that it forces us to live a story. We have been forced into this life by the breath of God. We come out crying and gasping for air, and what we do with that air is what constitutes the quality of our story.

We can bemoan our unsolicited life all we want but when we do, we ruin our stories because we play the victim. We can rage at God for bringing us into a world we did not ask for, but when we do we play the villain.

There is no getting around the fact that we are living inside a story of our own making. This, however, can be a terrific challenge if we choose to see it that way.

A PATH TO MEANING

If we look closely, we see in stories a path we can take to live a more meaningful life. The path, if taken rightly, guides us through a heroic journey into and through a transformation in which we become a guide to others.

There are more than a few good books about the hero's journey. There have been many more written about experiencing a sense of meaning. What hasn't been written is a book that breaks this journey down into a practical process.

The truth is, our lives can be charged with meaning, just as a good story is charged with meaning. Good stories, however, obey certain rules. Stories are built on age-old principles, and when storytellers ignore those principles, their stories suffer.

If you have ever felt like your story is so uninteresting you don't even want to turn the page, there is hope. Even a casual exploration of the principles that make a story meaningful can deliver a better life experience.

As my own story began to get better, I noted many of the principles that were causing the improvement and about ten years ago turned those principles into a life plan and daily planner.

Since creating my life plan and performing the morning ritual of filling out my daily planner, I've maintained that strong sense of meaning. Life has not been perfect, and I've not always been happy, but in the ten years since I created my life plan and used the daily planner, I've never failed to wake up interested in my own story. I've written books, started a company, met a wonderful woman, and am starting a family. I'm late to the family game, but better late than never.

Regardless, I used to not like life, and now I do. Even with its injustices and tragedies, it is a beautiful experience, and we get to participate in making it so. One of the great tragedies a person can experience is to feel dispassionate about their own life. To wake up believing fate is writing a terrible story that we are bound to is akin to being imprisoned in our own skin.

The idea that fate writes our story is a lie. We do not suffer fate. We partner with fate to write a story generated from our own God-given creativity and agency. And that story can be more than interesting: it can be meaningful.

The rest of this book will explore how.

2

·············

A Hero Accepts
Their Own Agency

For an unfortunate number of years, I ignored the idea my life could be better. I rejected the idea I needed to create structure and a rhythm. And ignoring those ideas cost me a great deal. I'd say ignoring the fact I needed to take control of my own life cost me an entire decade of personal progress.

If I could go back, I'd take my life more seriously. Specifically, I'd take my work more seriously. I'd live with some discipline.

Back then, though, I was entirely controlled by moods. I only wrote when I was emotionally ready. I'd wander Portland all day, going from coffee shop to coffee shop, listening to music on my headphones, trying to muster up the mood to write the next paragraph. There were seasons, and I'm not exaggerating, when I'd spend up to three days trying to find an inspiring feeling so I could write the next page of whatever book I was working on.

I remember a certain chair at Common Grounds Coffeehouse on Hawthorne. I wrote a good page there one morning and came to believe the good words would only come if I were sitting in that chair. For the better half of a month I'd show up in the morning, and if somebody was sitting in that chair I'd go next door and eat breakfast tacos at the table by the window until whoever had been sitting in that chair left the coffee shop.

I know all this sounds like the writer's life, but career writers don't live this way. Stephen King and Annie Dillard and James Patterson treat writing as a discipline. They clock in like blue-collar workers and build their books brick by brick.

All my wandering around searching for a mood was a victim mindset. Victims live at the mercy of forces outside themselves. Back when I lived in Portland, it was as though my writing life was entirely controlled by the weather patterns of emotions. It's a wonder I ever finished a book at all.

Again, heroes are not as strong as you think. They are usually unwilling to act, in need of help, filled with self-doubt, and often incompetent in the very area in which they are given a challenge.

The journey, of course, changes them. Still, the hero must participate. They must decide to take the journey. Bilbo leaves the Shire. Ulysses sets sail. Romeo scales the wall into Juliet's courtyard. At some point in a story, the characters divide, and it becomes obvious who will be the victim, who will be the hero, who will be the villain, and who will be the guide.

I'd never have been able to accurately put words to it, but during the season of frustration with my roommates, a seed had been planted. I needed to change. I needed to take my life seriously and practice some discipline.

The heroic transformation begins when the hero takes responsibility for their life and for their story. The hero becomes the hero only when they decide to accept the facts of their life and respond with courage.

I understand the fear of trying, though. As I said, I was reluctant to embrace structure. Thinking of myself as a victim offered me one thing that a heroic mindset couldn't provide: an excuse.

I think that's the big reason for the lack of transformation in the life of a victim. When we think of ourselves as a victim, we get to stop trying because we believe we are helpless.

When I talk about victim mindset, I'm not talking about actual victims, of course. Actual victims really are hopeless. They are trapped in a dungeon, beaten, and abused; truly they have no way out. At no point in my twenties was I an actual victim. I just wanted to think of myself as a victim, so I wouldn't have to try.

I often wonder if people pray for rescue and then resent God for not helping them, only to realize, in time, that God did not rescue them because they did not need to be rescued. They were not actually victims.

THE LOCUS OF CONTROL

Psychologists have a name for the act of surrendering power to outside forces. It's called an "external locus of control." It means that the person surrendering power believes external forces are in charge. An internal locus of control means we believe that, to a large degree, we are actually in control of our own destinies. But an external locus of control means we believe we are helpless to outside forces.

This is an important transition for all of us to make. Psychologists have associated an external locus of control with higher levels of anxiety, higher rates of depression, lower wages, and troubled relationships.

An internal locus of control, on the other hand, has been shown to correlate with a stronger sense of belonging, less depression, higher wages, and more fulfilling relationships.

These correlations make sense. A person who does not believe they can control their life is a back-seat driver in their own skin, sliding around as "fate" blindly swerves off the road. They do not realize they are actually in the driver's seat and can steer their life toward preferred outcomes.

BUT HOW MUCH OF OUR LIVES CAN WE ACTUALLY CONTROL?

The truth is, of course, we cannot control every aspect of our lives. I do not get to control the weather (though I do get to decide whether or not I stand in the rain) and I don't get to control other people, at least not if I want a healthy relationship with them. I don't get to control when or where I was born, my height, whether or not I have a good singing voice, and so on.

But some people mistakenly believe that because they cannot control some characteristics of their lives, they cannot control their lives at all. Corporations, politicians, and even some religious leaders often take advantage of these people. Manipulative leaders try to convince you that your problems are not your fault and if you just trust in them or their ideology, you'll be okay.

Social scientists use another term to explain the dynamic of personal control and power: *agency*.

Agency refers to the ability we have to make our own choices. And all of us have agency. Agency can be unfairly limited by factors such as social class, religion, and ability, but agency is almost never limited completely. In fact, very happy people know a secret: a human being has a ridiculous amount of personal agency. A person's reaction to a set of circumstances dramatically affects how their story plays out.

Looking back on my life, I know exactly where I forfeited my agency. I'd given it up as a kid. My father left us when I was two, and my mother went back to work. Without a college degree, she worked as a secretary at an oil refinery. She left early in the morning for work, so my sister and I walked to school, often in clothes our mother had sewn because we couldn't afford new clothes. I found comfort in food and would eat anything sugary. I started gaining weight and was, without question, the heaviest kid in school. All this of course led to me being bullied on the playground.

When you're bullied you have two choices: you can fight back, or you can lie down and play dead. I lay down and played dead. And to a great degree it worked. If I was helpless, nobody bothered me. I learned to stay helpless, and worse, I actually believed the lie that I was helpless.

Certainly those were difficult times and I have grace for my past. But remember, there's a point in every story where the characters divide. The character who becomes the victim believes they are helpless and acts out of that belief. The character who becomes the hero accepts their agency and rises up against their circumstances.

What I lament about my life is how long it took me to accept agency. If I'd had the knowledge to make that transition earlier, many years could have been redeemed. I'd have had a lot more fun in my teens and twenties if I'd risen up.

In fact, growing up poor, walking to school, and feeling a little neglected didn't have to be such a bad thing. I wish I had been as proud of my upbringing then as I am today. My mother worked hard. She loved us enough to sew our clothes. We had it tough, but when you have it tough you learn to get tough, if you are willing. It just took me a lot longer to be willing.

BUT WHAT IF WE REALLY ARE VICTIMS?

What I lament even more is that I spent time playing the role of victim while there were actual victims in the world.

My wife serves as chairman of the board for an organization called Rescue Freedom. Rescue Freedom helps survivors of human trafficking escape, find safety, and recover from their trauma to live healthy lives filled with meaning. It's a truly beautiful organization.

When I think about actual victims, I think about the children Rescue Freedom helps. It's embarrassing that I once viewed myself as helpless when I was not helpless. In fact, even the survivors of human trafficking that Rescue Freedom helps are never referred to as victims. They are referred to as *survivors*. Because that's what they are. These children are strong. They are heroes who needed some help to rise up against their oppressors. They are characters in a story with a bright and shining future. They are not charity.

True victims can easily turn into heroes once they are set free. In fact, former victims who are now heroic survivors are some of the strongest, most courageous advocates for change because they know firsthand the oppression and pain that exists in the world.

My favorite philosopher, Viktor Frankl, is a terrific example of a real victim who, through sheer strength of will, summoned the heroic energy to transform himself to live an incredible story.

In the 1930s, his therapy, called logotherapy, began to invite people who saw themselves as victims into a life of meaning. Logotherapy translates into a therapy of meaning. Frankl used it to treat patients who were suicidal, and the treatment worked. Many of his patients experienced a positive transformation as they began to work on projects, join communities, and consciously reframe their pain to see it as a benefit. He taught his patients to realize their own agency.

Frankl's theory about life having meaning even in the midst of extreme pain and suffering was tested and proven. The psychologist had been working hard on a manuscript explaining his theory when the Nazis invaded Vienna in 1938. As a Jew, he was taken captive. Before he was taken, though, his wife, Tilly, sewed his manuscript into the lining of his coat so he could continue his work. On day one in the concentration camp, his coat and manuscript were taken. His work was lost.

The Nazis then separated the psychologist from Tilly, who was pregnant with their first child. She was then murdered in the camps, along with his unborn child. Frankl would soon learn that his mother and father had been murdered too. He was understandingly despondent and near suicidal himself.

Instead of taking his life, though, he realized his life could still have a purpose. He accepted agency over what he could still control and somehow, even in the camps, began rewriting the manuscript in his mind. Even amidst the forced labor and death that surrounded him, he continued his work, not allowing his captors to take what remained of his agency.

In the camps, friends would come to him and challenge his notion that their lives had meaning, even as they were treated like animals.

"Our stories will be told and when they are told," Frankl explained, "the world will know there is an evil which must be protected against. Even if they kill us, our lives serve a purpose. Our lives have meaning."

After miraculously surviving the camps, Viktor Frankl would go on to lecture about how life offered a deep sense of meaning to any person who accepted the challenge. He encouraged audiences who felt a personal despair amidst hardships to reframe their own story. He encouraged the world to understand that, in all its light and dark, life was still beautiful, and we could contribute to the growth of that beauty.

He would rewrite his manuscript and publish the book. *Man's Search for Meaning,* Frankl's seminal work, would go on to sell more than sixteen million copies.

Paramount to Frankl's ideas is personal agency. He argues that it is our choice to believe life has meaning and that we can choose to experience that meaning if we structure our lives to serve a greater purpose.

No other thinker has helped me understand what I experienced in the transition from victim to hero more than Viktor Frankl. I write a great deal about story, and while the work of another scholar, Joseph Campbell, is remarkable and certainly helped me understand the elements of story and how they work to explain life, it was Frankl's thoughts on logotherapy that laid out my own hero's journey.

If Viktor Frankl did not see himself as a victim, I had no excuse. None of us do. We can each reframe our story and structure our lives in such a way that we experience a deep and fulfilling sense of meaning.

After realizing what victim mindset had cost me, I began writing with a greater purpose. I decided to dedicate the mornings to write, regardless of my mood.

I'd yet to create the defined structure for my life that I'll outline in this book, but I did decide I wanted to publish. And so I wrote a book. A publisher signed me, and I worked hard telling the story.

While writing my first book, I believed it would be a bestseller and my story of transformation would be complete. The book sold about thirty-seven copies and my mother bought twenty of them. It was a failure.

But if a hero does not experience setbacks, the story gets dull. Setbacks and challenges are the only elements in a story that change us. But I didn't know any of that then. I just thought I'd failed, and I got mad about it.

I'd done my part, after all. I'd shown up and disciplined myself to get the words down. Fate owed me a bestseller and dinner with Oprah.

The failure of that book launched another season of temptation. The shiny victim bait dangled in front of me. I had been wrong about my own talent. I'd worked for a year preparing a letter to the world that nobody wanted to read.

And so here was another point in my story where the characters divide. It was as though I could see the paths before me. I could choose to play the victim or the hero. The victim path offered me an excuse; it tempted me with the sympathy that others would offer. But knowing how tiring and empty that story was, I decided to take the better path.

I started looking at the bright side. Writing a book nobody had heard of made me an exceptional conversationalist at dinner parties.

"So you wrote a book? Can I find it at a bookstore?"

"It's not on the shelf. But if you ask the guy behind the counter, he can order it. And you can borrow it from the library, but I don't get paid for that."

I kept writing. The next book would sell well. I was still very overweight, though. When people lined up after my book readings, I asked whom to make the autograph out to with burger on my breath. I wore large sweaters even when it was warm. I was still absolutely terrible at attracting women. But somehow that made me come off as the underdog and readers liked that. At book readings people looked at me with hope, as though the part of them that binge eats ice cream while watching television could someday write a book too.

I kept trying. I lost some weight. I got a girlfriend and when that didn't work, I got another.

Then I began structuring my life with a little more discipline. Thanks to Frankl, plus a few other writers, and an ample amount of time studying the lint in my slowly shallowing belly button, I realized what I'd been searching for.

Frankl nailed it: I'd been searching for meaning.

His prescription for meaning was simple. In the next chapter I'll talk about it and how I experienced it. Essentially, though, it was to throw yourself into a story in which you try to accomplish something important. You accept the challenges and overcome them if you can.

I lost my victim mindset like I lost the weight: slowly, inconsistently, and often with setbacks. Still, if you want to lose twelve pounds in a year and only gain four back the following year, I can help. All you have to do is worry a lot. It takes a long time, but until you shed the weight you can wear a large sweater.

Meaning is the same. You accept your own agency. You move your locus of control from outside yourself to inside yourself. You go on intentional adventures, and you get to experience meaning. You have a goal, you overcome challenges, you put another page in the typewriter. You wake up each day and you push the plot forward. The more I lived intentionally, and the more focused my life plan and daily structure became, the more I transformed.

In the challenge of writing another book, I felt meaning. In the fear of talking to a girl at church, I felt meaning. In buying a puppy. In climbing a mountain. In learning to kayak, there is meaning.

It's more nuanced than that, but I trust you understand. To experience meaning, you have to accept the fact of your own agency and move into your life with intention.

The point is that life feels like it has meaning if you structure your life so that you experience it.

I began to realize that life and writing stories had some of the same rules. If the characters do not want something, do not face their challenges, and do not try hard things and grow, the story doesn't work.

If we don't want something, face our challenges, and try hard things, our life stories don't work, either.

I didn't fully know what those rules were just yet. I was still figuring them out. But I did realize that I had a great deal of control over my life, especially over my attitude. Again, I accepted the fact of my own agency. And my life slowly started coming together.

WHAT IF LIFE IS NOT MEANINGLESS?

Later that year, a friend's friend asked if we could get together to talk about writing. He was a young unpublished writer who had read one of my books and wanted to know how the publishing process worked. We sat and talked for a while, and I slowly realized he was a nihilist. He rejected the idea that life had meaning.

At one point, as he pontificated somewhat poetically about the great burden of his existence, I interrupted him.

"What if life is not meaningless?" I asked.

"What do you mean?" he asked.

"Well," I said, "what if life has meaning and you just have to live a certain way in order to experience that meaning? What if dialectical reasoning won't get you to the answer?"

"Explain," he said.

I should not have worded my response this way. But I said, "What if life itself is not meaningless? What if just *your* life is meaningless?"

We did not become friends after that, but I still think it's a valid observation.

What if life is like a story and you and I are in the theater of our own minds, looking out the cameras of our eyes, and the story unfolding feels either meaningful or meaningless based on what we decide to make happen in it? And what if, if we trust fate to write our stories, it feels meaningless, but if we accept our own agency and structure our lives a certain way, our lives become charged with meaning?

I don't think my answer was good enough for my friend's friend. I think he wanted proof that life had meaning before he was willing to experience that meaning.

But to me the whole idea that meaning can be experienced but not proved was making more and more sense. I could not explain why I was beginning to feel a greater sense of purpose or was more interested in stepping into my shoes every morning. I just knew meaning was happening.

And it all had to do with dreaming up a story and living into that story. It all had to do with living as a hero on a mission.

I believe there are millions who, when the story of their childhood and high school and college ends, sit in the empty theater of their mind, watching the credits roll, waiting for fate to tell them yet another story. But once we are on our own, our parents, our teachers, and our culture stop telling us what to do, and we have to dream something up for ourselves.

The term I now use to describe the restlessness of sitting in the theater of our minds waiting for something to happen is *narrative void*. No longer being interested in your own story, mainly because the story isn't interesting: that's how many people live. And it's sad.

This is what I had begun to understand. And I have come to believe it more every day for the past twenty years.

My life is no less difficult than anybody else's, and I am not always happy. But in answer to the question of whether my life feels charged with meaning, I say yes. It does.

Many stories didn't work out. Every good writer has thousands of pages they've tossed into the trash. Bad writing is bad writing. It's the same in life. Not every day works out.

But many of the stories I tried to live worked terrifically and I'm glad of that. Betsy and the coming baby. This book. My company. Our home. I'm not the same man I used to be because the stories I've chosen to live have transformed me into somebody else.

In stories, characters who try hard things transform. They have to. The person they were is not enough to overcome their challenges. They have to get stronger, humbler, more tender, smarter. They have to change in order to get over the wall.

And in the growing pains that come with transformation, there is an experience of meaning.

I can't prove it. But back then I began to feel it. And I still feel it today.

When we live as victims, we do not experience a deep sense of meaning, but when we live as characters acting on an important mission, we do.

So, how can we accept our own agency and live in such a way that we experience meaning? I'll tackle that in the next chapter.

3

....

A Hero Chooses
a Life of Meaning

FOR A LONG TIME I believed "meaning" was a philosophical idea that you experienced only when you agreed with a set of beliefs. I no longer believe this is true. In fact, I don't think meaning can be experienced by believing a set of ideas at all. Instead, I believe meaning is something you experience in motion.

Meaning is existential. To be more precise, it is an emotional state you experience under certain circumstances, and those circumstances can be created by us, and those circumstances are relatively easy to create.

To experience meaning, a person simply needs to rise up, point at the horizon, and, with deep conviction, decide to venture out toward the hope of a meaningful story. Meaning is something you experience while you are on an adventure.

Victims, then, cannot experience a deep sense of meaning. Victims are not in motion. They are not trying to accomplish something or build something or create a new world. Instead, they believe they are helpless. This is yet another reason I look back on my victim years and see them as a wasted season.

Today, I experience a deep sense of meaning and I'm glad. I spent years studying theology and philosophy. They were good years, but I was mistaken to believe that the study of meaning would give me a sense of meaning. Studying love does not cause you to fall in love. Falling in love happens under a certain set of circumstances.

Again, meaning is experienced by a person when they are moving forward into a story. And it's terrific news that this story can be one of our own making. We do not have to trust fate to write a story for us. We can write that story ourselves.

And yet all of this begs a question: What are the rules we must follow to experience a deep sense of meaning?

A FORMULA TO CREATE MEANING

As I've already mentioned, I'm a fan of Dr. Viktor Frankl. I've spoken and written about his work for years because, in many ways, he saved my life. Or at least he dramatically improved the quality of my life.

I discovered Viktor Frankl on a particular day in which I was most likely to receive and understand his ideas.

About fifteen years ago, I joined several friends on a bicycle journey across America. It took us the majority of a summer. We started in Los Angeles and finished in Delaware.

This was early on in my transformation from victim to hero. At the time, I was just starting to come out of my victim shell. My self-identity was just beginning to transform from victim mindset to hero mindset, but I was still clunky in the living. Regardless, I was starting to understand that life is best lived in motion. I'd published a few books and was proving I had mental stamina, but my body was still mush. I signed up for the bike ride because I wanted to see if I could become a character who did hard, physical things.

The ride was definitely a hard, physical thing. America is a large country, especially when you cross it horizontally, without an engine. Surprisingly, though, I enjoyed the challenge. In ways, it was seven weeks of forced meditation. I found comfort in the rhythm of my bike pedals flowing over each other. The trillion fence posts along America's back roads and the cows that ran away from us, spooked at the sound of the ball bearings in our gears, offered a subtle anchoring to the earth. The big weather that came at us from across the deserts gave us the feeling we shared the world with friendly and not-so-friendly monsters.

We were definitely living inside a story. Flat tires. Hailstorms. Heat exhaustion. Wipeouts. Trying to find food. Trying to find water. Every day getting another hundred miles in, however we could. There was meaning in those miles. We were characters heading east, believing if we kept pedaling, an ocean would appear and tell us we had transformed, that we were the kind of people who could do a hard thing.

And yet for the final week of the ride, I had an uneasy feeling of concern. I was worried because I'd noticed something over the previous decade: when I set out on an adventure I felt a sense of meaning, but when it ended (such as when a new book came out, a big speaking opportunity was fulfilled, or when I got into a relationship) I'd crash. After I accomplished anything good, the sense of meaning seemed to decline. And it declined rapidly.

Some of my saddest, most depressing, *can't get out of bed* experiences have come in the season following a significant accomplishment.

MEANING HAPPENS WHEN YOU GET A STORY GOING

I now know that when a story ends and the credits roll, you've got to get a new story going.

What I was feeling in those final days of the ride across America was the ramifications of the end of a pursuit, the flickering end of a story. I lay in bed a few nights before our last day thinking about how great it was going to be to ride across Delaware and walk into the Atlantic. And yet I knew there would be a temptation to sit there too long. There'd be a temptation to stretch out the moment of accomplishment, to sit and stare at a blank page rather than slip another sheet of paper into the typewriter and get another story going.

We took a day off in D.C. before the final push. We rode around the National Mall. We were fast, in very good shape. We went from the White House to the Capitol and then to George-town in minutes. We weaved between taxis and buses, keeping up with traffic and even passing the slower cars as their brake lights clogged up at intersections. I'd never been in such good shape and have never been since. It was the first time in my life that I experienced the thrill of a body that worked well.

It was in a bookstore in D.C. that I discovered Viktor Frankl's *Man's Search for Meaning.*

The title seemed bold, and it also seemed like an answer to my concern. I'd certainly experienced meaning on the ride across America, but I found myself wondering how to keep that sense of meaning going.

I'd heard of his book but had never read it. Knowing I'd need a read for the flight home, I picked it up.

The next day was thrilling. We rode seventy-five miles in just over three hours. Delaware is flat and small, and from D.C. you can get to the ocean fast. And we were fast. The mountains and the deserts and the headwinds and the blister-ing sun were behind us. The adrenaline of a story coming to an end fueled our legs. Ten miles from the Atlantic, we took off our helmets to better feel the ocean air. I think all of us cried. The tall grasses on either side of the road waved us in—and then there it was. Big as a bathtub for the cosmos. The Atlantic Ocean. We walked our bikes to the shore, dropped them in the sand, and swam.

We swam for a long time, hardly believing we'd done it.

And yet, the whole time I knew tomorrow or the next day or the day after that, the ghost of meaninglessness would begin to haunt me. It's okay to rest. It's good to rest. But you cannot stay down for long. Even after a great adventure, we must all dream up something new.

I could hear the still, small voice of the ghost: *Meaning is only experienced in motion.*

On the flight home, Viktor Frankl gave me a name for the restlessness. He called it the "existential vacuum." He accurately named the state that we get ourselves into when we finish an adventure only to sit in the theater of our own minds, watching a blank screen. "Existential vacuum" felt like the appropriate term.

I now believe the "existential vacuum" is where many people live. It's that feeling that life should be better, more interesting, more fun, more rewarding, and more fulfilling.

Viktor Frankl was right. All the good characteristics life offers can and should happen. In fact, he had been a prominent neurologist and psychiatrist in Vienna during the 1930s, a couple of decades after Sigmund Freud popularized psychoanalysis by espousing that the desire for pleasure motivated human behavior. Frankl disagreed with Freud. Frankl said man did not have a will to pleasure, but a will to meaning. And when man couldn't find meaning, he distracted himself with pleasure.

Why are we so restless? Because ice cream is distracting but not fulfilling. Because alcohol offers a fabricated sense of peace. Because lust is not love.

Frankl was right. *We distract ourselves with pleasure when we can't find a sense of meaning.*

THE FORMULA FOR A LIFE OF MEANING

Frankl's formula to experience a life of meaning was pragmatic and threefold:

1. Take action creating a work or performing a deed.
2. Experience something or encounter someone that you find captivating and that pulls you out of yourself.

3. Have an optimistic attitude toward the inevitable challenges and suffering you will experience in life.

As I read *Man's Search for Meaning*, thinking through the trip we'd just taken across the country and the deep sense of meaning that had come with the effort, I realized all three elements were present. We had a specific ambition: to ride our bikes from the Pacific to the Atlantic. We were also experiencing something beautiful that was more interesting to us than ourselves: one another, not to mention the landscape. Pedaling across Joshua Tree at sunrise. Climbing the long, slow mountains on the Blue Ridge Parkway. Then, finally, the challenges: every day was painful, but the pain served a purpose. The pain was making us stronger by creating a rich closeness that only comes when you share a challenge with friends.

The entire trip, much like the books I'd written or projects I'd completed, had a little story to it. Without knowing it, all of us on that trip had lived like heroes on a mission. We'd thrown ourselves into logotherapy and as such experienced a deep sense of meaning.

But the big revelation for me came when I realized that just because you experience meaning while living a story doesn't mean it sticks around. If any of those three elements are removed, you stop feeling a sense of meaning and return to the existential vacuum.

Many people live in the existential vacuum without realizing they can easily experience meaning again. They just have to get a little story going and lean into that story.

Think about the most restless, uneasy seasons of your life. Were you fascinated by a project that demanded your attention? Were you mesmerized by the beauty and the people around you? And were you able to reflect on your suffering and identify how, while it was certainly painful, it was also enriching your life?

If any of those three elements were missing, the sense of meaning likely dried up and you were left staring into your belly button, holding the lint up to the light and asking silly questions like *Why are we here?* and *Why is life so empty?*

Frankl's formula—that meaning was found by taking action on a project, being enamored by something or someone outside yourself, and giving your pain a purpose—has been accidentally stumbled upon by all of us at various times in our lives.

But for me the big revelation came when I realized we could cause meaning to happen any time we wanted.

In other words, human beings have the ability to make meaning.

If we choose a project to work on; if we open ourselves up to the beauty of art, nature, and even other people; and then if we can find a redemptive perspective for our inevitable pain, we will experience a deep sense of meaning.

WHAT DOES MEANING FEEL LIKE?

To me, meaning does not feel like joy or even pleasure. I've had plenty of bad days in the midst of experiencing meaning. Meaning is better than that. Meaning feels like purpose. When I experience meaning, my life feels as though it is playing an important role in an important story. I have never been able to prove that sense of purpose is justified, but it hardly matters. When I am experiencing meaning, it *feels* as though my life is a story that is interesting to myself and also good for the world.

I have plenty of friends who espouse religious or philosophical ideas in an attempt to prove life has meaning; yet they do not experience meaning in their lives because they have not set out on a story.

How many people sit in church pews hearing lectures about God only to return home and feel restless? And why? Perhaps it is because we do not experience meaning by studying meaning. Rather, we experience meaning by taking action. Even Jesus said *follow Me* rather than *figure Me out*. What if the experience of meaning requires action?

Additionally, it's my belief that meaning is philosophically and theologically agnostic. You can be an atheist, a Christian, a Muslim, or anything else and experience meaning, just as you can be an atheist, a Christian, or a Muslim and experience joy and love.

Meaning is not an idea to be agreed with. It is a feeling you get when you live as a hero on a mission. And it cannot be experienced without taking action and living into a story.

In the years after I learned how to make meaning, it was fun to meet others who were experiencing meaning too. I could recognize them immediately. They were building a family or a company. They were leading a team. They were trying to write a book or record an album or create enough art for a gallery showing. They were in motion. They were building something.

Not only this, but they also combined their ambition with an appreciation for challenge. They were not victims. They knew that pain was part of life, and they knew they could use pain to help them transform into better versions of themselves. After all, we are all going to experience pain—why not allow it to improve our character and our outlook on life?

Finally, they were not self-absorbed. Instead, they were fascinated by the world, by art and music and nature. They were focused on their projects too; on the beauty they believed they were bringing into the world.

And because they were characters inside a story about building something and being useful, they experienced meaning as well as transformation.

I have found that "my people"—the people I click most with in this world—are not people who agree with my religious ideas or even my political ideas, but rather people who are living as characters inside a story of their own making.

WE CAN DECIDE TO EXPERIENCE MEANING

Somewhere in this season of my life, I began to get a little obsessed with designing my life so I could experience the most meaning. I began to live more strategically. I planned my life the way a writer plans a story: I defined an ambition (just as a writer does for their lead character), I embraced challenges, I learned from mistakes, and every day I'd try to put a little something on the plot. Again, I did all this in such a way as to optimize and stay within the experience of meaning.

Everything didn't go perfectly for me. As I said, we can't control every aspect of life. But we get lucky a great deal more when we stay in motion. I controlled the projects I worked on, the attitude I had about conflict, and the community I created. I controlled the books I wrote, the schedule I kept, the discipline to get up early every morning. I lived with intention.

What I noticed, then, is that life tends to meet you as you get moving; and the more you move, the more opportunities life throws your way.

To make living a life of meaning easier, I created the life plan I'll lay out for you later in the book. I also created a simple daily planner to keep me on track. The way I viewed the life plan was similar to how a writer views the outline of their story. They plan their book, then they write it. If the outline needs to change because the book flows differently than they thought it would, that's fine, but by creating an outline they established a direction and cultivated the inspiration to start writing. The daily planner, then, became my little secret to staying disciplined. If I filled out my daily planner page on a given day, I was always, always more in tune with my own story than if I didn't.

The daily planner and life plan helped me lay three big ideas over the top of one another: The first was Viktor Frankl's formula for how to experience meaning. The second was all I'd learned studying the four major characters that are in almost every story and how playing those characters affects the quality of our lives. The third was the need to apply all I'd learned to life itself and take advantage of the incredible (and ever expiring) opportunity to create meaning.

The idea that we'd all do well to live like heroes on a mission didn't come to me until later, but the realization that I needed to proactively move into life rather than simply let life happen to me was enough to improve my overall experience.

It is true my life plan changed, over time. Each year I'd edit my life plan a little bit based on the slightly new direction that both my desires and the opportunities life handed me seemed to offer. Nevertheless, without the exercise of creating a life plan, my story would have devolved in entropy and ultimately a narrative void. The existential vacuum.

I've been using the life plan I created for about ten years now, and each year seems to have gotten better.

As I said, to create my life plan, I went back to the three elements Frankl described in his formula for meaning:

1. *To create a work or do a deed.* Life invites us to be important and necessary. If we wake up each day and have a task to accomplish, especially a task in which other people are involved or without which other people might somehow suffer, we become necessary in the world. We sense we have a purpose (because we do). By requiring a work or a deed, I think Frankl was saying: *Get yourself a great reason to wake up and get out of bed in the morning. If you do, it will help you avoid the existential vacuum.*

2. *To experience something or encounter someone.* We should acknowledge that we are not alone in the world and in fact the world and the stories unfolding upon it inspire awe. We all know the greatest experiences we have in life are dramatically enhanced if they are shared with others. According to Frankl, to experience meaning, we should get involved with a small group of people we love and who love us, or we should find something that invites our focus

beyond ourselves to the beauty of the world around us. A lone walk through the forest is good for the soul just as a trip to a gallery can offer inspiration and a sense of mental expansion. The point is this: encounter something that pulls you out of yourself so that your world becomes larger.

3. *To have the ability to choose a perspective toward any set of circumstances, including challenges and suffering.* While I've found each of the three elements of Frankl's formula helpful, it's this last one that helped me transform the most. Essentially, Frankl argued there was no negative event that could happen to us that could not be somehow redeemed. "Redeemed" is my word, not his, but I think it's fitting. By redeemed I mean that, as humans, we are able to take the most painful of tragedies and turn them into something meaningful. Frankl believed that while tragedies should be acknowledged and grieved, they can also produce something beneficial. This doesn't mean tragedies are good. Nobody wants or should have to experience a tragedy. It only means that from the ashes of our tragedies we can create something beautiful, and by creating something meaningful with our pain we begin the process of healing our wounds.

Another danger of victim mentality is that it does not allow us to redeem our pain. Those who see themselves as victims do not see the benefit of pain. While pain is often unbearable, it is also creating a strength, or a tenderness, or at the very least, a deeper understanding of the true nature of life: it's often difficult.

The benefits of pain should not be overlooked.

In stories, pain is the only way heroes transform into better versions of themselves. If you wrote a story about a hero who transformed, only you did not put that hero through a great deal of pain, the audience would not believe the transformation was authentic. They might accuse the writer of naïveté.

Intuitively, we all know that pain is the force that transforms us.

Frankl argued there was no challenge a person could experience in which that person could not find a redemptive perspective. That's a bold claim. Yet none of us can call the man naive.

When asked to answer the question of the meaning of the death his family and friends had experienced at the hands of the Nazis, Frankl answered that while what happened was pure torment and we should fight against such atrocities, the deaths of his wife, child, mother, father, and millions more served a purpose: they proved to the world the existence of evil.

While he did not wish for the deaths of six million Jews, he did not want the story to end in the great deficit that often happens with tragedy. He meant his counsel as a proclamation: the deaths of the Jews in Europe will serve a meaningful purpose, that is, as a warning to the world.

The need to redeem our pain is not only true on a global, epic scale, but on a personal scale as well.

We must take the thing that has hurt us and shape it into an inner strength, perhaps even into a prevention of that thing ever happening again.

To me, this idea is paramount if we are to transform from victim to hero. A victim wallows in their pain while a hero picks it up and turns it into something useful for themselves and others.

Of course, what we are really talking about when we talk about transforming from victim to hero is *healing*.

Victims heal into heroes and heroes strengthen into guides.

My friend Allison Fallon is a good writer. She and I have a little side project going. It's called *Write Your Story*. In our little workshop we teach people to reflect on something in their lives they've overcome. Then we ask them to reflect on who they were before the challenge and who they became because of the challenge. Then we teach them to write that story in about five pages, following a specific story formula.

Sitting and processing your own challenges and realizing how much they have transformed you should be a necessary exercise in every high school. When you sit and think about what you've been through and how strong your challenges have made you, you enter into an improved identity. You realize you are stronger than you knew and you also realize you are interesting.

Nearly everybody has overcome something very difficult and in doing so been given the opportunity to transform. Few people, however, fully actualize their transformation because they stay stuck in their old identity. You have to sit and realize all that you've overcome in order to believe your strength. The villain inside you will belittle the hero inside you to no good end. Processing your own story shuts the mouth of the villain.

Part of my life plan, years ago, involved building a home on a piece of land with a large carriage house where people could meet and also a guest house for people to come and find rest. I didn't just want to build a home, I wanted to build a place from which community would grow. I shared that vision with Betsy and we entered into the story. We've built that home now, and the carriage house too. The guest house is still being built but will be done shortly after this book comes out. We call the place Goose Hill, named after our chocolate Lab, Lucy Goose, because Lucy has always loved life and has always loved people. People ask me all the time what my favorite part of the place is, and I always tell them it's the bookshelves in the carriage house. In the carriage house we built floor-to-ceiling shelves along the back wall. After people write their stories, I will three-hole punch them and put them in binders on those shelves. I want my daughter to grow up in a place where she's constantly reminded of what a person can do with their life. If any of our guests ever want to be inspired, they can just go up to the carriage house and read about all the things people have overcome and the beautiful ways those challenges have transformed them. Today the shelves in the carriage house are empty, but as we invite people to write about what they've overcome and how that challenge transformed them, those shelves will be filled with volumes of encouragement and inspiration for anybody who wants to sit and read them.

Pain can serve a purpose if we cause it to. Again, while we do not have power over all that happens in the world, we do have power over our perspective. We can choose to take unfair and undue pain and cause it to serve our own story so that we become better. So that we transform.

While Frankl certainly would have chosen his wife and child's lives over the lesson their deaths taught the world, he did not believe they died in vain. Their lives and even their deaths served a purpose.

MEANING IS SOMETHING WE CREATE EVERY DAY

Victims and villains do not create meaning for themselves or for the world. Heroes and guides do. We build lives of meaning by stating an ambition, by enduring challenges, and by sharing our lives with others.

When the long bike ride was officially over, I knew I needed to dream up another adventure. I needed to take action, share that action with others, and accept the inevitable challenges involved in the new ambition because those challenges would stimulate growth.

When I got home from Delaware, I felt it happening. I'd sit restlessly on the couch watching the Tour de France on television. My legs needed to move and so did my mind. I'd get up and ride fifty miles just to feel normal. I was eating nearly ten thousand calories per day because my metabolism was still racing from the cross-country ride. I decided I couldn't just sit around. Depression was closing in. I felt the existential vacuum breathing on the back of my neck.

Only a month later, I found myself traveling the country supporting a candidate for president. I served as a surrogate speaker and spoke to groups about the issue of fatherlessness and how the candidate, who happened to be from a different political party than the one to which I belonged, had the best plan.

These days I don't identify as a Democrat or Republican and honestly believe the two parties have caused too much damage and polarization to offset the benefit of their proposed agendas. Nevertheless, the candidate I supported back then won the White House. A year later, I found myself on a presidential advisory council, helping to write a book-sized consideration of presidential objectives that might dignify fatherhood in a culture that seemed to slowly be vilifying men.

That's another story, but as it relates to my thesis here, I did not experience a crash after our bike ride. I avoided the narrative void. Instead of losing a sense of meaning, I simply found a new story on the campaign trail. I found a certain meaning and even a thrill sleeping on airplanes, trying to get wrinkles out of my shirt in airport bathrooms, and sleeping in the back seat of a car as a small group of friends and I traveled through swing states with our message.

Over the coming years, the president would implement every idea we came up with. Father's Day at the White House became a major event to showcase the importance of fathers in the lives of children. He elevated nonprofit organizations working to reunite incarcerated fathers with their children, giving them even more of a reason to stay out of prison. Federal funding was allotted to mentoring programs.

I was proud of the work we did, but it wasn't all altruism. I also got something from the work. I got to avoid the existential vacuum that happens when we let fate write our stories. I got to avoid the crash and burn.

While I was on the campaign trail, the text messages started coming in from my friends who'd ridden their bikes across the country. The physical toll on all of us was mesmerizing. Our bodies were in chaos. And so were our minds. Many struggled with anxiety and depression, and all of us wished we were back together, pedaling from the Atlantic back to the Pacific. We all joked about meeting at that beach and heading back in the opposite direction.

What was happening, though, is something that happens to a lot of us. A story had ended and a new one had to begin. For most of us, growing up was a fun story. Then we lived a story in high school, then college, then marriage, then kids, and then, well, nothing. At some point life stops handing us prewritten cultural scripts. The credits roll. And few people ever figure out that they've got to create a story of their own in order to find narrative traction. At some point life takes the training wheels off and forces you to create a story that is better than the restless boredom that comes by trusting fate.

Midlife crisis happens when the cultural scripts end but we fail to write a new story for ourselves.

The point is, when a story ends, another has to begin. And if we want the story to wake us up from a sense of meaninglessness, it must include the three elements Viktor Frankl set out as a formula for meaning.

If you live with the intention I've laid out in this chapter, life will feel different. It will feel as though you have a purpose in this world.

I'll spend the rest of this book walking you through the paradigm shifts I've realized and even showing you the tools I've created to plan your life and organize your time in order to experience meaning.

After the bike ride and the political campaign, I formalized my life plan and daily planner page. In the ten years I've used the tool, I've not lost the sense of meaning. And I consider that sense of meaning a saving grace. The tools I created are available at the back of this book or you can scan the QR code to get a digital printout of the Hero on a Mission (HOAM) Life Plan and Daily Planner. My team has also turned the life plan and daily planner into online software that allows you to experience the tools in the context of community. You can actually get updates from friends who've accomplished important tasks and you can read through their life plan if they've marked it as open to the public. The process has been helpful for thousands, and I love getting letters and emails from people who've found it transformative.

In full disclosure, the printout of the life plan is free, but the software has a small fee associated that is used to employ our developers, keep it updated, and build improvements. Still, the entire process is in this book. If you finish the book, you will fully understand how to create a life of meaning.

OUR STORIES CAN PROVE LIFE HAS MEANING

Does life have meaning? I believe it does. You have to admit there are times when the absurd beauty of the human experience gives you pause. What a sky can do with a sunset. What a songwriter can do with a guitar. For me, our baby moving in Betsy's belly. The garden we keep in the backyard. A good poem. A good meal. Yes, life is challenging and has tragic elements, but it is also beautiful. And meaningful. It is meaningful because we make it so.

Viktor Frankl used to say it is not our right to question whether or not life has meaning, rather it is life that questions us: Will you make your life meaningful or will you suffer the existential vacuum?

The other day a theologian friend came to town, and we took a walk. I've known Julie for a long time, since we were kids.

I love it when we get a chance to catch up. Back when I was single, she and her husband invited me on a Greek Orthodox pilgrimage around northern England. The time we didn't spend sitting in lectures, we spent drinking tea and mining the problems of the soul, trying to figure out whether there was some bit of theology that would lead to wholeness, or, more important, why the last bit of theological revelation we'd come to hadn't produced a sense of wholeness.

This time, however, the conversation felt different. I'd not taken a walk with Julie in nearly ten years. As we talked about the state of the church and the state of our culture, I found myself less interested in mining the depths of philosophy or theology for answers. I even texted Julie later to say something had changed in what I wanted in life. I no longer wanted answers. Instead, I accepted life on its terms, with all its unanswered questions and yet wanted to take advantage of its invitation to experience meaning. This is not to say I do not have beliefs. I consider myself a spiritual person and pray daily. But I don't really want any more answers. The search for definitive answers has often led to tense and sometimes futile conversations. I'd rather be grateful than all-knowing. Julie texted back that she'd had some of the same revelations. She said we were in a similar place. Julie is a renowned theologian. She studies, for sure. I trust what she meant by saying we were in a similar place is that these days she studies more out of curiosity and a desire for a relationship with God than she does to feed an insatiable desire for answers and certainty.

Growing up, I used to sing along with Bono as he cried out that he still hadn't found what he was looking for. I still sing along with Bono, but it feels different now. I still haven't found what I'm looking for either, but having discovered a deep sense of meaning I am now uninterested in the search for anything else. I am fulfilled, even in the unknowing. I do not want to live life looking for something I don't have. I want to become more and more interested in the opportunities I've been given.

In short, I am pleasantly distracted by meaning.

So how do we live a life of meaning? Again: First we define an ambition. We choose something we want to bring into the world, or we join a community or movement that is bringing something into the world. Second, we share our experience with others, and we allow ourselves to become interested in the people and beauty that exist outside ourselves. And third, we accept challenges and even tragedies as a fact. Of course we try to prevent them, but we do not wallow in pity when they occur. Challenges are painful, but they can serve a purpose if we allow them to.

I've come to think of this lifestyle as living as a hero on a mission.

I fear even as I type that phrase and use it as the title for this book, it rings of arrogance, as though somehow those of us who live this way are heroes and others are not. But it bears repeating: heroes are not perfect creatures. Often, in fact, they are weak, unwilling to act, afraid, and in desperate need of help.

The single characteristic that sets heroes apart, however, is that they are willing to accept a challenge that will ultimately transform them. Heroes take action, which is why they are so good at experiencing meaning.

Every hero in every story you have ever loved wanted something specific and was willing to sacrifice to get it. Every hero in every story you have ever loved experienced pain and setbacks but found a perspective that allowed them to keep going. And every hero in every story you have ever loved wanted to serve a purpose larger than themselves.

And because they stepped into a story, they experienced a transformation. At the end of the story, they were a better person than they were at the beginning.

I have experienced transformation, and I'm hoping an ongoing transformation continues to define my life. Amidst the false starts, the fear, and the need for help, I know if a person keeps moving into new and exciting stories, they will change for the better.

Healthy people grow. Healthy people transform.

4

....

What Elements
Are Necessary for a
Person to Transform?

HAVE YOU EVER GOTTEN together with a friend from years back and, after talking, realized they hadn't changed at all? By that I mean they tell the same jokes, relive the same stories, struggle with the same problems?

The reason it feels odd to encounter a person who has not changed is because human beings are designed to change, and when we don't, it's an indication that something is wrong.

As a memoirist I did a lot of reflecting. I wrote about my fears and insecurities and even my failures. I wrote six or seven books in that same voice, hopefully chronicling my changes. I confess it's sometimes embarrassing to think about all I wrote about back then. I don't have any copies of my own books in my house. Or at least I don't have any that I know about. For me, yesterday is yesterday and I'd much rather live for today and tomorrow. Regardless, the reason I don't go back and read my old stuff is because I find myself nearly unrecognizable. I still agree with most of the ideas, but I find the whining and complaining I did in my old books to be annoying. This isn't a confession of shame. I'm proud of the kid who wrote those books, but I'm also proud that that kid got better.

In the past ten years I've transitioned to writing business books. I write with more authority because I believe in myself more than I used to. Occasionally somebody will comment that they miss the old Don. But honestly I don't miss the old me. The old me was heavier, lonelier, more bitter, and terrible at relationships.

The way I look at it, I got healthier. Healthy people acquire discipline and learn from their mistakes. These are the qualities that lead to change. I can't write books like I used to because I'm not the same person I used to be.

Sometimes people don't want you to change because it requires too much mental work to recategorize you in their brain. They want you to stay dumb and slow and safe. The old you wasn't a threat in their social construct. But I think every healthy thing changes and unhealthy things stay the same. I say go ahead and transform and just let others get used to it. It won't take long for them to appreciate you for who you've become and give you a new space and more respected space in their mind.

I like what the stories I've lived have done to me. I'm not perfect but I'm a lot better than I was. After all, if the therapy doesn't work, why the heck are we paying so much for it? The therapy worked pretty well for me, as did the self-reflection necessary to write all those books. I'm different now. I'll take this version of Don over the previous one any day. He's happier.

So why do some people change while others stay the same? Why do some people get stuck and others get unstuck?

LIVING A STORY IS THE ONLY WAY TO TRANSFORM

Most of the stories we love are about characters who transform. The hero usually begins their journey as an unwilling participant, not yet ready to take action. But when Gandalf tells Bilbo about the ring, or Katniss stands in for her sister in the Hunger Games, they are forced into the story through an inciting incident. These incidents exist in stories because they exist in life. Something—or more accurately, a series of somethings—happens to us. We are forced to act. We leave home, fall in love, or get our hearts broken. Our house burns down. Our car won't start. We win the lottery. We lose everything in a bad investment. These incidents offer us a challenge, and it's through accepting these challenges that we transform. It's through these challenges that a positive evolution begins to take place. These challenges allow us to prove ourselves to ourselves and to the world.

When something difficult happens, victims accept defeat but heroes ask, "What does this make possible?"

Show me a person successful in business and I'll show you somebody who learned from their failures. Show me a man who is grateful for his wife, and I'll show you a man who had his heart broken a few times.

Our pain and our challenges chisel us into better versions of ourselves. For sure, the blow of the chisel hurts. But the result, if we allow it to be, is a sculpted character competent to create a better world for themselves and others.

THE HERO MUST WANT SOMETHING

It does not take an inciting incident, though, to get a story going. All it takes is a little curiosity. A hero starts wondering what it would be like to accomplish X, or to build Y.

I think one of the reasons people do not change is because they do not leave the shire.

Many of us have stopped wanting things in our lives. We've killed our desire. When something didn't work out, we mistakenly believed that nothing else would. And perhaps we came to believe that by not wanting anything we could mitigate all risk of failure. Not wanting something, after all, is a form of self-protection. Instead of trying, we play it safe.

I believe this is a sad reality for many. A story has to be about a character who wants something. At any point in a movie, the audience should know what the hero wants. She wants to top-ple the regime, he wants to win the tournament, she wants to rebuild the home she lost in the flood. The hero must leave their comfortable life and pursue something risky. The hero has to want something, and she must take action to get it. Oth-erwise the story fails to gain narrative traction.

That brings up another characteristic that leads to transfor-mation: the hero must want something *specific*.

A story about a person who wants fulfillment sounds boring for a reason. What is that story even about? We all want fulfill-ment. What's so special about this guy and what sort of fulfill-ment is he looking for?

Defining something elusive to head toward will have us right back in the existential vacuum. If we want to be happy, life will never work. We have to want something that will make us happy, and that something needs to be defined specifically so it posits a story question in our mind. Will we be able to run the marathon this spring? Will we start that rafting company? Will we sell the house and buy a farm?

A storyteller must define an exact thing the hero wants. They want to win the karate tournament. They want to save their father's company. They want to marry their sweetheart.

Once the hero defines what they want, the story begins. And why does the story begin? Because, again, when a hero defines what they want, a story question is posited. The audience, and for that matter the hero, is engaged by a single interesting ques-tion: Will the hero get what they want?

When an audience can't determine what a hero wants, or when what the hero wants is too elusive for an audience to understand, the audience loses interest and becomes bored.

This is yet another warning for those of us who want to side-step the narrative void. If you don't want anything, you aren't living inside a compelling narrative. When we don't want any-thing, or, perhaps, when we cannot exactly define what we want, we become characters in a story with no plot.

Let's not pretend that not wanting something is somehow restful. Not wanting anything can be emotionally grueling. Imagine sitting in the theater of your own mind and not knowing what you want, having to watch a confusing story day after day about a muddled character who floats here and there like a twig on water.

When we don't want anything, not only do we lose interest in our own lives, but we cause others to lose interest in us. I've never read a story about a princess saying she dreams about meeting a handsome young man who rides up on a white horse and tells her he doesn't want anything.

My guess is she'd rather marry the horse.

As Frankl said, we must have a project on which we are willing to take action. And when that deed is done, we must have another. And then another. It's by wanting something that we enter into life and engage its challenges. And it is through engaging in these challenges that we transform.

What we want hardly matters. We do not find meaning in the wanting; we find meaning in the pursuit of the thing we want.

As long as what we want is good for us and good for the world, we will have at least one element that it takes to experience a deep sense of meaning. Whether we want to win a dance contest or compose a symphony, start a business or build a family, it's the thing we want to bring into the world that invites us into life itself.

So, what do we do if we don't want anything? I've met a lot of people who have this problem. But then I start asking them what they enjoy. They enjoy music. They enjoy gardening. They love their family. The truth is, they want a lot of things; they just haven't sat down and put a compelling vision for their life into words.

Do you love music, gardening, and family? Start a family band and sing about vegetables at a local farmers market. Now that's an interesting story. I won't be buying the record, but cheers to you all the same.

The point is this: don't get stuck trying to pick the right ambition. Wondering what's the right thing to do is the same as having an external locus of control. The answer isn't out there. It's in you. And there isn't a single answer. There are a million answers. The only wrong answer is not to want anything. The right answer is to point to a specific spot on the horizon and start walking.

A HERO MUST ENGAGE THEIR CHALLENGES

Two more reasons people do not transform: they either avoid challenges or do not learn from them.

Again, though, conflict is the only way we change. Without pain, there can be no transformation.

In his lectures, Viktor Frankl posed a question to his audiences that went like this: If you look back over the hardest seasons of your life, would you choose to delete them if you could? Now that you are through them, would you not want to have lived them?

For most, the answer to this question was no, they would not want to delete the hard seasons from their memory. They would not have wished the painful season away. This is not always the case, of course. The loss of a child. Having made a decision that broke trust. There are times when we wish we could turn back the clock. But even in those instances, there was personal growth in our pain. When you decided to be disloyal, you learned of your own limitations, and it humbled you. When you made the mistake, you learned of your own fallibility and developed the strength of character required to live differently.

The only reason my company succeeds today is because of the losses I experienced early in business. After I became a bestselling author, I lost every penny of my savings in a short-term investment. I'd just sold my home in which I'd put my life savings. I put all the money into a venture and woke up one Monday morning to find out it was gone. I cried myself to sleep for at least a week. I never thought I'd see that much money again. I'd blown it.

But from that hard season I learned more about earning and managing money than I could have learned in a decade at Harvard. The pain caused me to start paying attention. And because I started paying attention, I grew a successful business. Now, every year, Betsy and I donate to charity at least the same amount of money I lost that Monday morning.

It wasn't just troubles with money that helped me grow stronger. I remember when I was much younger being on a flight from Chicago to Portland. I was so big I had to ask for a seatbelt extension. The person next to me grunted every time they moved, letting me know they didn't appreciate that I was taking up some of their seat.

I sat there feeling sorry for myself, but that pity never turned into ambition or action. Instead, I believed that if I felt sorry enough for myself, if I were enough of a sad sack of decomposing DNA, then somehow, some way, God would feel sorry for me and my problems would simply go away.

Living under the weight of all that pain did not transform me. Year after year I stayed the same. Again, in stories, victims don't transform. They are the same characters at the end that they were at the beginning. In stories, victims play a bit part: they make the hero look good and the villain look bad. But they do not change. They do not get stronger. Their problems do not simply go away.

What I didn't realize then is that the pain isn't there to crush us. It's there to invite us to become stronger.

It wasn't until I got help that I began climbing the mountain under which I'd lain for so long and transitioned from victim mindset to hero mindset. I started to exercise. I started to eat much better. I started to slowly lose the weight. I started to change. Part of the reason I started to change is because I entered into stories that required me to lose weight. A story about losing weight is one thing, but a story about riding a bike across the country necessitates getting into shape. When a story demands transformation, you are much more likely to transform.

Viktor Frankl even reasoned that pain was part of life by design, that suffering was life's way of questioning us and even developing us.

But what do we do with an injustice? We do not let it overwhelm us. Instead, we redeem it; we use that evil intention to transform us into better versions of ourselves. Again, the temptation to manifest victim energy is what we must avoid.

"You get bitter," a friend once told me, "or you get better."

What if life is not designed to be a joy ride? What if we are not here to be entertained? What if, instead, life was a noble duty?

If we begin our day believing life is supposed to be easy, we will certainly have a terrible day. Life is not easy, nor was it ever supposed to be.

Life is often fun and entertaining, but that's not the point of it. The point of life is to live a great story and experience meaning, and that often involves engaging challenges.

We have a responsibility to engage this world with courage. In many ways, engaging life with courage is our duty. And it's by embracing that duty that we find fulfillment and meaning.

Rabindranath Tagore's poem says it best:

> I slept and dreamt
> that life was joy.
> I awoke and saw
> that life was duty.
> I worked—and behold,
> duty was joy.

A HERO LEARNS FROM THEIR MISTAKES AND MISFORTUNE

We have all met another kind of person, one who makes the same mistakes over and over. They enter into a community and make good friends, then they do something like borrow money from those friends and fail to pay the money back. When they are confronted, they play the victim rather than account for their actions. They do not accept responsibility. The community becomes frustrated; they know they are being used. Then the person leaves the community and enters into another community only to borrow more money, fail to pay it back, and burn another bridge.

How in the world can a person make the same mistakes over and over and not learn?

For me, learning from my mistakes begins with turning off the ego and being willing to admit I actually make mistakes. My ideas could be wrong. My attitude could be toxic. The problem in my world may very well be me.

Until we are willing to admit we make mistakes, we will never learn from our mistakes.

Still, it confounds me that some people cannot admit fault. It is as though their security is threatened if they admit that they have done something wrong. Regardless, these people are not our problem. They will have to deal with the consequences of their own egos and continue moving into new communities to start over.

For the rest of us, failure is an education. Mistakes are an education. Wrong deeds can even be an education.

When we see mistakes as a curriculum rather than a judgment, the velocity in which we transform increases. Failure, pain, mistakes, and even injustices directed against us offer an advantage—if we let them.

So how does a hero transform? They define a specific ambition for their lives, they engage challenges rather than avoid them, and they learn from their mistakes and misfortune.

TRANSFORMATION IS THE NATURAL PATH

Transformation is natural. None of us look the same as we did when we were babies, and when we are old, we'll look very different than we did when we were middle aged.

Things that are healthy and alive change. The converse is also true: things that are dead do not change. A rock does not change because a rock is not alive.

Change is caused by us wanting something and being willing to engage in the challenges of achieving what we want.

Before we want something, though, we may have to deal with another problem: there may be some part of us that believes we shouldn't want anything at all.

There are people who do not dream of a brighter future for themselves and others.

There are people who believe they do not deserve anything in this life. And worse, there are people who do not want anything because they do not want to stand out. For them, survival means blending in.

But to not want anything, in my opinion, is to not want to participate in the story of life. And that is akin to not accepting a gift from God.

In order to create our life plan and make use of the daily planner I'll show you later, we are going to have to decide to want something.

Whenever I sit down to write a story, I start with a character. I imagine that character and then I ask myself a single question that will determine where the story goes: What does the hero want?

This is one of my favorite questions to ask a new acquaintance. After the small talk, of course, when the conversation gets more serious, I love to ask, "What are you trying to build? What are you bringing into the world that wasn't there before?"

If they have a great answer to that question, and sometimes they do, I know I'm in the presence of a hero on a mission.

5

. . . .

A Hero Knows
What They Want

LATER IN THE BOOK I'll be helping you create your life plan. In order to create that plan, though, you're going to have to define some kind of ambition for your life. You're going to have to want something.

In a story, a hero wants something. They want to win the championship or disarm the bomb. They want to slay the dragon or win the spelling bee.

If a hero doesn't want something, the story fails to start. The reason we like stories, in fact, is because they posit a story question that is interesting enough to hold our attention for a couple hours or a couple hundred pages.

If we aren't sure what we want in life, there is no story question in our lives either. And if there is no story question inviting us to take action, we will lose interest in our own lives.

Narrative traction happens when we get interested in a story and lean in to see what happens. Most people do not have narrative traction in their own lives. They find their lives boring and uninteresting, so they scroll through Instagram feeling jealous of those who seem to be living a captivating life.

But when you are interested in your own story, the stories of others are not so threatening. They get to live interesting lives and so do you.

Again, in order to experience narrative traction in our lives, we have to want something. Or some things. When we want something, we have a reason to get out of bed and engage the challenges that stand between it and us. And of course it's those challenges that transform us.

If you think about it, all action is motivated by the opening and closing of story loops. I wanted to date Betsy, so I took a risk and asked her out. I wanted to write this book, so I took a chance and wrote a sentence and then another.

The story questions these ambitions brought me then created a kind of narrative traction that kept me interested in my own life. Is this the woman I will build a family with? Will this book be any good?

If we don't want anything, then we can't get the story started and we run the risk of losing interest in our own lives.

For some, wanting something specific in life can be troublesome.

There are people who find it difficult to want things. Perhaps they grew up being taught resources were scarce and if they want something in life they are by definition taking something from somebody else.

Others, perhaps, were raised by their parents to want certain things, maybe a high-paying job or a strict, religious devotion. But when they got older, they discovered they didn't want those things at all. Now they are confused about what they should want.

Still others want so many things and have so many options that they feel paralyzed by the idea of making a choice.

While it's true a hero must want something for a story to get started, it's also true that no one has an ethical responsibility to want something. We are each free to live the way we wish.

That said, if a hero doesn't want anything, their story cannot engage an audience. I also believe that if a person doesn't want anything, it will be difficult for them to maintain an interest in their own life, and it will also be difficult to experience meaning.

And while experiencing meaning is not a moral obligation by any stretch, it's certainly a nice way to live. Sitting around pulling lint our of our belly buttons isn't a very interesting thing to do with our lives. That story gets boring and makes us restless quickly.

A HERO IS NOT ASHAMED TO WANT SOMETHING

A person's reasoning for wanting nothing in life might go like this: *When people want things, it ruins the environment and leads to murder, pillage, and deceit. I do not want to be one of those people, so I don't want to want anything.*

But not wanting anything because some people want unhealthy things is not a sufficient answer, nor does it address the world's problems. Let's not pretend not wanting anything is somehow noble. Knowing there are starving people in the world and "not wanting" to help them is the plotline of a terrible story. There are plenty of noble and even moral reasons to want something in this life. All human advancement has happened because a person or group of people wanted something.

I read a book once by a man who espoused a perverted version of Buddhism, claiming all our yuppie troubles would disappear if we quashed our every desire and simply stopped wanting things. But let's consider his perspective.

The words you are reading exist because centuries ago people wanted to connect with one another through the written word. Our schools exist because people wanted to learn. Our economy exists because people wanted opportunity. The wheel exists because people wanted to make work easier. Roads exist because people wanted to travel. Courts exist because people wanted justice. Homes exist because people wanted shelter.

The only reason this man was able to write a book telling people not to want anything is because it was printed using words that were read by people who had learned to read, published by a company, sold in exchange for money, transported by trucks that had wheels on roads that had been built by people who wanted to travel. Even the man's copyright through which he could legally receive royalties and buy a home was defended by courts created by people who longed for justice.

Wanting to create something new in the world is not bad. Wanting bad things is bad.

A HERO WANTS SOMETHING MUTUALLY BENEFICIAL

None of us have entirely pure motives.

We like to think life is clean, that people are either good or bad. That is yet another reason some people have trouble wanting anything. They sense that some of their motives aren't entirely altruistic, so they shut down their ambitions.

In reality, though, progress is made when what we want is mutually beneficial for ourselves and others. If we are honest about nearly every "charitable deed" we perform, we will admit we get a little pleasure out of being a charitable person. I don't believe there is anything wrong with that.

The reason I started a business coaching company was to help small businesses learn how to grow. And also because I grew up poor and feel insecure about my self-worth. I work hard to not be poor. Is that noble? I give myself a B– on nobility. Regardless, were I not driven by my insecurity about having grown up poor, I would not have been quite as motivated to start a company, and thousands of small businesses wouldn't have the help they need.

Mixed motives are what fueled me. If you're honest with yourself, you'll admit they fuel you too.

Here's a complicated sentence: I love my wife unconditionally because I think she's beautiful and because she loves me back; therefore, I do not love my wife unconditionally.

I think those of us who believe our motives are entirely pure are a bit delusional.

So, here's where writing stories and living stories differs: in stories, characters often need to be clean; either all villain or all victim or all hero or all guide. But you and I will never, ever operate in such purity. We will always have some victim and villain flowing through our veins. You will never be as selfless as you want to be.

The truth is, while you are motivated to serve others, you are also motivated to serve yourself.

That's why when it comes to figuring out what kind of story we want to live, we should look for something that is mutually beneficial.

If it sounds to you like I'm saying to live a life of mixed motives, it is because that's what I am actually saying. You read me correctly. I don't believe you will ever have entirely pure motives. If you say you do, I don't believe you and don't believe you are self-aware. Forgive my judgment, I just think God lives in heaven and that we mere mortals are fallen creatures. And I think it's high time we accept that we aren't perfect.

Many people won't take action at all because they do not want to pursue anything that feels selfish or greedy. I understand that. Our selfishness should be kept in check. But don't forget, if you have mixed motives for feeding the hungry, the hungry still get to eat and I don't think they really care about your motives.

If you pay close attention to stories, you'll find heroes to be incredibly flawed. They often have primitive desires and do selfish things. They are not always brave, and they do not always help the people around them. And yet, they try. They struggle with their base desires in order to become better. That's why we fall in love with them.

A HERO WANTS TO SHARE

In fact, if a hero comes off as perfect, we begin to think of them as self-righteous. We don't tend to like characters who think "they are better than us."

There is a sweet spot, though: a character who is relatable and yet altruistic at the same time. They want something for themselves but don't want to hoard what they acquire. They want to share.

The truth is, I am more motivated to accept challenges and do hard things if the project benefits me and also benefits somebody else, preferably somebody I care about.

If I do things only for me, it feels too selfish. If I do things only for others, I start feeling a little hungry for personal reward. But if I do things that are mutually beneficial, I hit my stride.

For us to find that inner desire and identify something we want, we must discover something that taps into a deep drive within us. Once we find whatever that is, something we've always wanted to prove or some experience we've always wanted to have or some self-expression we've always wanted to create, we have to figure out how we can incorporate generosity into the mix, so our story doesn't get too cockeyed in the living.

Mixed motives. Trust me, becoming friends with your mixed motives is a good thing. Realize that your lesser motives will get you going, and your more elevated motives will make the experience beneficial to others.

The general rule is that a hero does not have to be perfect; they just have to consistently transform into a better version of themselves.

My favorite movie is *It's a Wonderful Life,* the story of George Bailey who, guided around his small town by an angel, is shown the world as it would have existed had he never been born. And it turns out a world without George Bailey is dark. His wife never finds love, his kids never come into existence, and the people of Bedford Falls can't afford good housing because his bank never lent them money.

We've all seen the film. But next time you watch it, notice how kind George is and also how rude he is. Notice how calm he is but also how frustrated he gets at the kids and the neighbors and the newel post that keeps coming off the railing on the stairs. He loses patience with his children. He barks at his wife. He demeans a coworker. In other words, notice how normal he is, how mixed his motives are, and how much you love him even though he is human.

George Bailey's life didn't have such a powerful impact because he was perfect, but because he was a flawed man trying to bring something good into the world.

Don't think you have to transform before you live a great story. Live a great story and the story itself will transform you.

A HERO IS IN TOUCH WITH THEIR PRIMAL DESIRES

In determining what motivates us, getting in touch with some primal drives can help. Is there something we are trying to prove to ourselves and the world? Is there something we enjoy or something that brings us pleasure? How do we want to be perceived by others?

These sound like intensely selfish questions. But I'm taking a risk here on being honest with you. Nearly all great accomplishments in the world have happened because somebody had mixed motives about doing the right thing.

When I talk about primal desires, I mean the desire to be financially independent. Or become known. Or win an award. Or experience passion. Or look tough. Or be perceived as beautiful or sexy.

If I'm brutally honest, one of the reasons I have succeeded in business is because I have a chip on my shoulder. I'm not proud of it, but there is still a part of me that feels embarrassed about having stood in line with my family for government cheese. I am still that kid who wants the rich kids at school to accept me as one of them.

Perhaps that's a sad motivation to make money, but that's one of the biggest motivations that fueled my work ethic. I wanted to be seen as important.

That said, what did that primal desire fuel? It fueled the building of a business that created many jobs. It fueled provision for a family. It fueled a company that teaches other business owners how to scale their own companies. In short, it fueled a terrific life for me and others. And in a very strange way, the primary desire helped me heal. It was my success in business that helped me prove myself to myself and others. Success allowed me to begin to heal the wound within. It felt good to prove to myself that I was willing to work very hard. And more than this, experiencing a little success helped me realize how shallow my desires to be rich actually were. It taught me that superficial success has a limited ability to provide fulfillment. It was only after I proved myself that I began to invest deeper in relationships and in helping others.

Life is not a journey about feigning perfection. It's about becoming better versions of ourselves.

People who are not honest about their nuanced motives are driven by the most deceptive desire of all: they want to believe they are perfect. In truth, they want to believe they are better than you. And there is nothing selfless about that.

Once we decide on a direction or project that motivates us, we need to figure out how to make our pursuit mutually beneficial. Is what we want something we can leverage for good? Who else will benefit from what we want to build? Will what we accomplish help resolve an injustice? If we accomplish it, will others think we are too selfish or self-centered? And if so, what can we add to our story to mitigate some of our selfishness?

It may sound odd to talk about our primal desires in the same sentence as our altruistic desires, but screenwriters have to deal with the nuanced ambitions of their heroes all the time.

The last time I went to a movie about a boxer who wanted to prove himself and win a heavyweight fight (who cares what the movie was—there are a million of them), the writers had to first define what the boxer wanted (to win the fight) and then spend an hour telling us what a kind and selfless human being the boxer was; otherwise, we wouldn't care if he won. I nearly rolled my eyes when, after tutoring a child and paying a single mother's rent and buying a homeless man dinner, the guy actually adopted a rescue dog. Why? All so we would like him and cheer when he finally won the final fight, which, spoiler, he did, only to make eye contact with the woman he helped, the man he helped, the kid he helped, and then the dog. Roll credits.

The more selfish the hero's ambition is, the more storytellers have to doctor up the script to make them look less like a jerk.

The lesson for us in all this is that while we are fueled by nuanced desires, we should make sure we discipline ourselves to do good things, be good to people, give generously, and mitigate some of the selfish desires that operate within us.

In real life, the more mutually beneficial your desire is, the more intrinsic meaning the story will have. Finding some kind of primal desire that will fuel you is critical in your pursuit of narrative traction and ultimately the experience of meaning. I'm talking about a deep drive within you that wants to build something for yourself. Then, figure out how to use that desire to make the world a better, kinder, more beautiful, and benevolent place. Otherwise, you'll have to adopt a dog.

A HERO MAKES A CHOICE ABOUT WHAT THEY WANT

Here's another rule about stories that will help each of us live a more meaningful life: try not to want too many things.

If it ruins our story to not want anything, it also ruins our story to want too many things, not because it's wrong to want a lot of things but because when we want too many things, the story itself gets muddled.

If Jason Bourne had wanted to know who he really was and also lose thirty pounds and run a marathon and marry a woman and perhaps adopt a cat but do so responsibly because he travels for work, the movie would have lost its plot and the audience would have walked away dissatisfied.

A storyteller has to make choices. In life, heroes on a mission also have to make choices. After filmmakers edit a movie, there are often as many scenes on the cutting-room floor as there are in the film itself. An editor knows that an audience cannot follow a story that isn't clean.

Having to pare down what I want has been a painful process for me. I love writing business books, but I also want to write fiction. The problem is, I don't want to write bad fiction; I want to write good fiction. If I'm honest with myself, I know it will take me at least ten years to hone my skills as a novelist. And when I number my days, I realize I don't have time. I cannot do both. I also want to run for office, but I want to build my company too. I want a lot of things that conflict with each other and so I know I have to choose.

I made choices. I left some opportunities on the cutting-room floor and took action on what I could actually accomplish.

To some, that last paragraph will sound like a compromise, as though writing fiction is a holy pursuit and writing business books is carnal. Of course, I don't believe that's true. It's just that I sensed I had two callings, not one. There were two paths, and I knew I'd love both. Having grown up poor and knowing how much all of my literary heroes struggled with money (and for that matter with alcohol and relationships), I chose the path that offered emotional fulfillment as well as financial opportunity.

In plotting our lives, there will be compromises. There will be unfulfilled desires. And that's a tension we will have to learn to live with.

Yes, you could have married somebody else, but you didn't. Storytellers make choices and they commit to those choices.

A HERO IS GUIDED BY A CONTROLLING IDEA

Again, when writing a story, the storyteller must make decisions. Usually, this involves defining a theme even before the story gets started.

The theme of the story is basically what the story is about. Some storytellers call it a "controlling idea" or the "moral of the story," but regardless, it serves as a filter.

The theme of *Romeo and Juliet* is likely something like "love is worth dying for," and the theme of *It's a Wonderful Life* is something like "a life of quiet kindness can have a powerful impact."

To choose something you want in life, try starting with your theme. My theme is to "pave a path for anybody who wants to experience a deep sense of meaning." That theme guides most of my life. My house, my books, my family, and my company all serve that theme.

When I help people create their life plan, I always start with their controlling idea. As we talk, the theme usually becomes obvious, at least to me. They value living in the moment. Or they value hard work. Or they value relationships over money.

Once we find their theme, we start dreaming about what they can do with their lives.

Your theme does not have to be permanent. In fact, as you get older, your theme may change. My theme when I was younger was likely something about getting the most out of life. When I got older, it was about learning a craft. Now it's about leveraging my experience for the benefit of others.

Our theme will change the deeper we get into our stories. Stories do have chapters, after all.

The great thing about assigning a theme to this portion of your life is that your theme, or your "controlling idea," will serve as a filter.

At some point in your life, you may begin to have too many great directions ahead, too many options. Your theme will help you figure out what to take action on and what to leave behind.

Without a theme, a writer may be tempted to include too many scenes, characters, and plot twists in their story. This will ruin the story. A story needs to be about something and that something needs to have definition.

When we get into the life plan later in this book, you'll develop a theme for the current year you are in as well as your five-year vision and your ten-year vision.

Once you know your theme, you will have a filter that will help you leave a few scenes on the cutting-room floor. When you define a specific destination for your life, your story will begin to take shape and you'll become more interested in your own life.

A HERO FINDS A STORY THAT STICKS

Not every mission "sticks." I've known plenty of people who decide they want to run a marathon only to give up after a few weeks. I don't judge them. The point of becoming a hero on a mission is to experience a deep sense of meaning, not to finish a marathon. If a person tries at something and doesn't like it, I've no more judgment for them than if a person starts to read a book or watch a movie and decides not to finish it because they find themselves bored.

In fact, the sooner you abandon a story that doesn't interest you, the sooner you can find one that does.

The key here is not to accept the fact you are a quitter, but to find a passion that won't allow you to quit. When you know what your life is about, and you know what you want to pursue, I assure you that you will get up early, you will swim across the river, you will walk through snow barefoot. Find the story you want to live and you won't have to worry about discipline.

There are times I get tired of people on Instagram showing us their muscles or their private plane talking about how we should be more disciplined. Those people have what they have because they've found a story they love, a story that makes the sacrifice feel good. Discipline is a good bit easier to come by if you've got narrative traction in your life. Rather than sitting around feeling ashamed of our lack of discipline, we'd do better to find a story in which we are willing to engage our challenges.

For me, the story of being a writer stuck. I have no choice but to write. If I were not paid to write, I'd write anyway. If you locked me in a jail cell with no pen or pencil, I'd write in my head. There are times when I don't feel like writing, but the desire to see what I can put on a page that day compels me to write anyway.

My books have helped me build an incredible life. I wrote memoirs then business books. One day I may finally write that novel. The written word is in me just like something is in you. What is that thing that you just have to do? It should guide your story.

I should also say becoming a writer is not the most fulfilling thing that has happened to me. Having a good career is nice, but our stories don't have to be about professional accomplishment. All my life I've wanted to write important books, work on important projects, and perhaps even become somebody important. The returns on those efforts have been fine but minimal. Absolutely nothing has made me feel more important than becoming a father. The second Emmeline was born, I knew without a doubt I was necessary. I never saw that coming. As the author Andy Stanley says, "Your greatest contribution to the world may not be something you do but someone you raise." I would add to that that the place you get the most meaning from life may not be in your accomplishments, but the necessary sacrifice you make on behalf of somebody else.

Meaning is centered in love: love for our projects, our world, our communities, and our families. We've got to find something that pulls us out of ourselves.

When our babies cry in the night and we are tired and dragging and wonder if we have lost our freedom, the answer is yes. We have lost our freedom. But we have gained meaning. Meaning costs something.

Regardless, when I work with people to help create their life plan, it's important to figure out what makes them happy.

The real question is: What are you endlessly curious about and does that curiosity draw you into a life of sacrifice? What will you give up your freedom to build?

A HERO ASKS, "WHAT IF?"

Sometimes when I'm writing a story and the plot seems stuck, I ask myself, "*What if?*" What if the hero falls in love? What if the hero gets caught up in a bank robbery? What if the hero discovers she can walk through walls?

What if? It's a terrific question to ask in order to overcome writer's block.

What if isn't a bad question to ask in life too. What if you quit your job? What if you lived in an RV for a year? What if you adopted a child?

What if is a question that leads to adventure. It gets you into a story that makes you excited to get up in the morning, and perhaps a little terrified.

Years ago I asked myself, "What if I wrote a book?" Then, after writing a few books, I asked myself, "What if I wrote a business book?" And then, "What if I created a learning and development company?" These days I ask myself, "What if I created a third way in the American political process?"

Asking *What if?* can drive incredible change in your life and give you a terrific reason to get out of bed in the morning.

A hero needs a "thing to do." If that thing is exciting and important, the hero will wake up feeling compelled to act. This is the essence of narrative traction.

A HERO CAN JOIN ANOTHER STORY

A hero doesn't always have to dream up their own story. It can be just as fulfilling to join somebody else's. I've done that plenty of times. Jumping into a presidential campaign, helping a friend write a book, riding a bicycle across the country—those adventures were dreamed up by others. I just signed the form, bought the gear, and headed out to join a group of crazy advocates.

The point is to start something or join something that creates narrative traction in our lives. Again, narrative traction is the feeling that our personal story is so interesting we can't turn away. We may not always like it, but we can't not do it. Even if it exhausts us and we find ourselves complaining about it, we're in it. The story has swallowed us up and is keeping us interested in our own lives

More often than not, joining a mission is even more exciting than dreaming up one of your own. There is nothing like becoming part of a group of people who are changing their world.

Here are the kinds of questions you want to start asking yourself as you begin to create your life plan: What will you build? What story will you join? What could your life look like one year, five years, and ten years from now?

6

. . . .

A Morning Ritual to Guide
and Direct Your Story

ONCE YOU DECIDE WHAT you want to do or build or join or create, you've taken the first step in becoming a hero on a mission: you've invited yourself into a story.

After you step into that story, you'll exit what Viktor Frankl called the existential vacuum. The reason this happens is because life is now asking you a question that requires action to answer.

Will you decide to work remotely and take your family on a yearlong trip around the world? Will you write that book? Will you start a community garden? And moreover, how will it all work out?

The story question is the magic ingredient that keeps you interested in your own life. And the action you take to answer that question pulls you out of the narrative void.

What story questions are creating narrative traction in your life?

All stories are built around the story question. Will the team win the championship? Will the couple fall in love and live happily ever after? Will the hero disarm the bomb?

Again, the story itself doesn't matter all that much as long as it poses a question. And that question must be so compelling that you are willing to change the trajectory of your life to make the preferred answer happen.

After we decide what we want, the next challenge is to see the ambition through to its conclusion.

But seeing things through is a challenge in and of itself.

The hard thing about reading a book like this is that we get inspired and feel great about life, and then find ourselves right back in the sea of distractions. A year later, we sadly realize we haven't moved forward on our story.

To make a story happen, we have to get up every day and "put something on the plot." That's the exact phrase I used the entire time I was starting my writing career. I'd get up in the morning, go down to the local coffee shop, and "put something on the plot." More recently, it's the phrase I use as Betsy and I build Goose Hill, our home that functions as a kind of mini retreat center for friends and family. It's the phrase I used as I built my company, and it's the phrase I used every morning when riding across America (sometimes with an expletive mixed in).

Talking about all these stories is easy, of course. Living them is hard.

The process of living a story (or, for that matter, writing one) can feel overwhelming. During Ernest Hemingway's early writing days in Paris, he used to stand at his apartment window looking down over the city and say to himself, "Do not worry. You have always written before, and you will write now. All you have to do is write one true sentence. Write the truest sentence that you know." With that in mind, he'd sit down and add another line to his legacy.

The stories we live seem romantic in hindsight, but in the moment, it's all work. When we are trying to live these stories we are attacked by the fear that things won't work or we are just not in the mood to put a little something on the plot. It's the constant interruptions and diversions and other people thinking we are a little crazy that cause us to stall in our stories and return to the narrative void.

But we have to keep going. We have to keep putting a little something on the plot, day after day, if we're going to find the narrative traction necessary to get us interested in our own lives.

What we need is a tool to help us stay on track.

For more than ten years I have been performing a simple morning ritual that channels my focus and intensity. The ritual involves reviewing my life plan and then filling out a daily planner page. Regardless of how foggy my mind is, my ritual changes the way I see the world. My morning ritual gives me clarity about what my story is about, why it's important, and what I need to do that day to put something on the plot. With that clarity, I start my day.

The ritual goes like this:

1. *I read my eulogy.* Yes, I've already written my eulogy, and every morning that I perform my ritual, I read it. I got this idea from Stephen Covey. It benefits me to read my eulogy because it helps me start with the end in mind. In a coming chapter, I'll show you my eulogy. I'll explain how I wrote it and how it helps center me as I start my day.

2. *I read my ten-year, five-year, and one-year visions for my life.* In the life plan I've included later in this book are three pages that, in a way, set my life in motion to become the sort of person I read about in my eulogy. Not unlike a professional golfer lines up her putt to roll over a line of specks on the green so her ball finds the hole, I use my one-, five-, and ten-year vision pages to direct my life at a closer range.

3. *I read my goal-setting worksheets.* I read about the three goals I am currently working on. Each serves as a sort of brick in the wall for my overall life plan. I only give myself three goals at a time because it's hard for a human brain to prioritize more than three projects.

4. *I fill out my daily planner page.* I created this page more than ten years ago but kept it mostly private until I decided to write this book. I credit this planner page with keeping me focused and driving a moderate level of intensity. If I were to reverse engineer any success I've achieved, I'd credit this tool.

A HERO DOES NOT LOSE THE PLOT IN THEIR STORY

The sure sign of an amateur writer is that as they write their story they lose the plot. When you're reading a book written by an amateur, you start out excited, wondering how the heroic lead character will get the promotion, win the race, or disarm the bomb. But then the storyteller gets distracted by a side character and spends a few chapters talking about them without ever returning to the original plot about the hero facing a challenge. The story is ruined, and you lose interest.

When you read a book like that, you get confused. You wonder what it's about and whether the author knows what they are doing.

You have likely met people who have lost the plot in their own story, such as someone who is experiencing a midlife crisis. They are living inside a narrative void because their plot was hijacked by distractions. One morning they wake up and realize that they are a thousand miles down a road they never intended to travel.

But how did they lose the plot in the first place? By surrendering their personal agency to outside forces rather than determining their own story and living into it day after day.

How do we stop this from happening? We write down the story we want to live and then remind ourselves of it in a ritual we perform several mornings per week.

I credit my morning ritual for much of what I have been able to accomplish in the past ten years. And of course I credit reviewing my life plan in the morning for helping me live a story that delivers a deep experience of meaning.

When I review my life plan, I remind myself of the story questions life is asking me. Will I continue to help small businesses thrive? Will Betsy and I stay best friends for life? Will our home help people find rest? Will our baby grow up believing she can have a positive impact on the world?

These are some of the questions that drive my life. And I'm reminded of them every morning. After I remind myself of the story questions my life is attempting to answer, narrative traction is guaranteed. These questions are interesting enough to me that I want to wake up every day and put a little something on the plot.

Without the ritual of reading my life plan, I'd have lost the plot a long time ago.

A HERO MAKES LIVING INTENTIONALLY A HABIT

A professional writer makes writing a habit. I learned this from Jerry Seinfeld. Years ago, I watched a documentary about his career. In the film, he credited his success to the time he spent refining his act.

One morning while skipping his writing session and eating at a café, he watched as a group of construction workers crossed the street to go to work. Each of them had their hard hat and lunch cooler in hand. He then wondered why creative work should be any different from physical labor. If he woke up every day and went to work on his act, refining his jokes and building a new routine, what would happen to his career? Today, after decades of "clocking in" and putting in the hours, he's the most recognized comedian in the world.

Since hearing Jerry Seinfeld reflect on his work ethic, I've reserved the mornings for writing. There are few mornings when I don't sit down and put a few more paragraphs on the page.

A professional writer knows their time is going to be attacked. They have to lock down the hours it takes to finish the book and then show up to work when they said they would show up to work.

That is how I look at my day-to-day life. If I want to grow the company, complete the building of Goose Hill, finish my books, be a good husband and father, stay healthy, and so on, I'll have to put in the hours.

Dreaming does not do the work.

What I've found is by reviewing my life plan, I remember the plot I've determined for my life and I know what work requires my attention. Of course that plot changes from time to time. New ideas come to me. New opportunities arise. But the point is, I don't live my life by accident. For the most part, it goes in the direction I want it to go.

A victim has no plan. They are waiting for a rescuer. A villain has a plan for destruction and strategizes vengeance on a world that has hurt them. A hero creates a plan that is mutually beneficial for the world and sticks with it. A guide has lived a great life and turns around to help heroes find and live meaningful stories of their own.

The Hero on a Mission Life Plan is based on two ideas: the first is Viktor Frankl's logotherapy, and the second is the elements that drive an interesting story. This life plan is not about productivity, though it will certainly help you become more productive. This life plan is designed to help you experience a deep sense of meaning.

There are many life plans out there. I try to keep mine simple. I find that if something is simple, I'm more likely to stick with it.

For the past ten years, I've shared the life plan with close friends and family. Word got out and now there are thousands of people who have used the life plan and daily planner to guide their lives.

If you are looking for a way to gain more focus and are curious about creating a new story for your life, the Hero on a Mission Life Plan and Daily Planner will work. It's worked well for me.

The rest of this book will help you create a life plan that transforms you into a hero on a mission.

To download the life plan and daily planner pages in a separate document, scan the QR code below. You can also use the pages at the back of this book.

ACT
2

Create Your Life Plan

From this point on, the book will guide you through the creation of a life plan and also teach you to use the Hero on a Mission Daily Planner. You can either use the back pages of this book or print out the larger worksheet pages by scanning the QR code at the beginning of this book.

The life plan begins with the exercise of writing your eulogy. Several chapters of the book will help you imagine the life you want to live so that your eulogy invites you into a meaningful story and also creates a sense of urgency in your life.

You will also be guided through the ten-year, five-year, and one-year vision worksheets. These worksheets will help you begin to picture the life you want to live and help you take small steps toward an objective that matters.

Following your vision worksheets, you'll learn how to fill out goal-setting worksheets that use a few tools to increase the chances you'll achieve your goals. Finally, you'll learn how to fill out a daily planner page that brings the entire process together and keeps you on track every day you use it.

If you visit HeroOnAMission.com, you will find our online software that will allow you to create your life plan online and also join a community of thousands of others attempting to live lives of meaning. The software version includes videos in which I help you create your life plan and daily planner.

7

. . . .

A Eulogy Allows You to Look Back on Your Entire Life, Even Before It's Over

BESIDES MY WIFE, MY closest companion in life is a thirteen-year-old chocolate Lab. I brought Lucy home when she was only seven weeks old. I was a lonely bachelor at the time, well past the traditional window for marriage, and was becoming convinced I'd be a bachelor for life. It was Lucy who cured my loneliness.

Every morning when I lived in Portland, Lucy and I would take a walk by the Willamette River. We'd walk a mile down the water and a mile back, me throwing a tennis ball into the water for her to retrieve. I can still see her dropping the ball at my feet, digging a trench in the sand, and barking until I picked up the ball to throw it again. When she was tired enough to sleep at my feet, we'd return to the house. Then I'd write. There were days when walking Lucy would take hours. I didn't mind. Her energy did as much as the writing to make me feel alive.

If a creature can enjoy a river and a walk and a ball, I could enjoy a day of writing. Lucy reminded me that work could be play.

That was nearly fourteen years ago.

She doesn't chase balls anymore. Betsy and I let her swim in the pool just a few days ago, and the next morning she couldn't get up from her bed. Her hind legs are thin; she wobbles to stand. Lucy has taken her last swim.

Watching Lucy get old and prepare to transition from this life has caused me to wonder more and more about my own story. Am I living a story that is meaningful? Will the story I leave to my child be one they want to emulate, one that will help them experience a deep sense of meaning themselves?

Every cold morning this winter, Lucy has stood on the porch for a minute or more, looking down at the five steps between her and the yard. Her eyes, genetically sad to begin with, finally have reason. She seems to calculate each painful step it will take to find the yard and relieve herself. She slides both front feet down the first step, pulling her hind and tail behind her like a trailer. Her rear legs shake when she goes. She no longer kicks up grass with her back feet when she's done. Her nose lifts into the air and twitches as though she were reading news about faraway events. Finally, she turns back toward the porch and looks up at me. We both wonder whether she still has what it takes to climb back into the house where she will sleep away the day.

Betsy and I have consulted with our vet about when to let Lucy go. She's on an anti-inflammatory and the doctor says she is more tired than in pain, but that will change soon enough.

It is a sobering reality. And frightening. Stories must end. Children live in eternity as do puppies, but people and dogs die. How long do we have? I have two more Lucy life spans in me, maybe three. But I don't want any more dogs. I want this one and I want her to be around to watch the baby grow up, and I want us to walk along the river and then come home to write our stories. Forever.

I can hear Viktor Frankl in my ear, though, whispering: *We love more what we cannot keep.*

And none of us get to keep our lives. We have to leave them behind.

In some ways, I've learned more about life from Lucy than I've learned from a thousand books. I've learned to be excited when somebody comes to the door. I've learned exercise is fun, and naps are fundamental. I've learned it's okay to let people know when you are sad. I've learned to be loyal.

I've already mentioned that the house Betsy and I have built in Nashville is called Goose Hill. Lucy's nickname is Goose. We named the property after her to remind us to be excited when people come to the door, to treat people with loyalty and love, and also to enjoy food and take naps.

If my life tells a story like that, I'll be satisfied.

WE PASS OUR STORIES DOWN

Betsy and I have worked hard to have a good marriage, to be sure. We've learned what to argue about and what to let go. We've aligned our values. We don't want to fight about anything; we are sold on our vision for Goose Hill and the company. We agree on the basic rhythm of life. We work, we rest, and we play. Betsy told me before we got married that she didn't want to marry a workaholic. I took that to mean I needed to create stories in my life that weren't just about professional accomplishment, but also about family and travel and fun.

Betsy is accomplished in her own right, but she also taught me how to sit on a beach and read a book, something I never thought I would enjoy.

We know, though, things are about to change. As Emmeline grows, we've begun to wonder if the drama is coming. Will she like us? Will she fit in? Will she be able to sit on a beach and read a book?

I know all of this sounds like selfish admissions, but there it is. Betsy and I have a great life filled with beauty and meaning. We are a little afraid that that life is going to come to an end. Does anybody really get off this easy?

Emmeline was active from the first signs of pregnancy. Betsy was a swimmer in high school, and I swear Emmeline was doing flip turns in the womb. Betsy would put my hands on her stomach in the mornings and evenings and smile as the baby danced and kicked against her tummy.

"That child wants out," I said.

"Good thing you got knee surgery." Betsy laughed. "You're going to need good knees."

We know intuitively the next season won't be so much about enjoying each other and our romance as it will be about a very serious responsibility. Our partnership will have to evolve from enjoying each other to depending on each other to serve a greater purpose. We'll have to work together and pass along all we know about love and life to another who can then use what she learns to build a life of her own.

In fact, when Emmeline was born I got the feeling that I'd just been handed the greatest responsibility of my life. I never saw it coming, but for all my desire to be important and do important things, all it took was having a child.

They don't tell you how bright the lights in the operating room are before you go in. It's like a football field during the Super Bowl. It's all routine for the doctors, and you're glad. They'd done three C-sections that morning. Betsy was calm and I was steady. They sat me on a stool at her shoulder and I took her hand. There was a partition over which Betsy couldn't see, so I saw the baby first. Emmeline. I described her to Betsy. *She's beautiful, honey. She's gorgeous.* The doctor held her up to the light as though she'd walked up onto a stage. She was gray and pink, mouth agape, discovering air. Her cry called out like a terrified lamb. Her eyes were clinched closed. She was at once helpless and miraculous.

I stood up out of reflex, still holding Betsy's hand. The doctors cleaned her off and weighed her. Then I held her, mesmerized. How could so much change happen inside three souls in just an instant? I stared into her face as though it were a portal, a crystal ball conjuring all of our families, past, present, and future. The doctors measured her, then I placed her on Betsy's chest and the three of us cried together. Later, when Betsy and I talked about it, we admitted she looked nothing like we thought she would. She was instantly the love of our lives and yet a complete stranger.

About a minute into life, she snorted like a little piglet. Betsy and I laughed. *What a good party trick, little girl. You belong with us.*

Before you have a baby, people tell you they can't believe the hospital lets you take them home. *You need a driver's license to drive a car, but you don't need anything to raise a child,* they say. But when you're forty-nine and run a company and have your first child, you don't think that way at all. I was ready. I wanted to apply lean management strategies to her upbringing. I wanted to bring her home to Goose Hill where everything was safe.

Another thing I worried about before Emmeline's birth was that I'd lose my motivation to change the world. I was afraid I'd not want to write or work because I'd just want to be her dad. My friend Paul Burns said it wouldn't happen that way, though. He pointed out that I had begun to think about my legacy, and that would provide a new level of inspiration. He said my story and my name would mean something and I'd want to protect it because it would affect my kids.

In the weeks after we brought Emmeline home, that's what happened. I've never been the type to want to be remembered. But knowing this little girl lives with my name makes me want that name to mean something good.

Emmeline also got me thinking about how short life is. Or at least how short the rest of my life is going to be.

I've got about thirty years left. Maybe less. There's a chance I'll never meet my grandchildren. There's a chance Emmeline will be rightfully pulling away from her parents to break away on her own during the very season I pass away.

I know it's all cryptic to think about, but the truth is that as beautiful as life is, it's also temporary. We aren't here for long. The beauty of new life and the sadness of death are all around us.

Even before Emmeline was born, I started filming little videos, messages to her that she can watch when she's older. I showed her Goose Hill and how small all the new trees were when she was born. One day she might get married beneath those trees. She and the trees will have grown strong and beautiful together.

In my mind I can see her in her forties and fifties, going back to watch the messages her dad left behind. I make these videos because I don't want to have to leave her, ever. But this isn't possible. We all have to go and all we can actually leave behind are the stories we've lived, the stories our children and grandchildren get to tell about us. Every story must come to an end.

On the morning we brought Emmeline home from the hospital, I helped Betsy and her sister into the car. As the nurse and I were strapping the baby into the child seat, we heard a bloodcurdling scream from the next floor up in the parking garage. I looked at the nurse and confirmed she'd heard it too. The nurse stayed with Emmeline, and I took off running. As I rounded the corner at the top of the ramp, I saw a woman collapsed on the ground, sobbing. Two other women were with her, all of them crying. As I got closer and asked if they were okay, one of the women let me know they'd just received terrible news. They'd lost a loved one in the hospital. I held my hand over my heart and mouthed the words *I'm so sorry*. I helped them get the collapsed woman off the ground.

Walking back to the car was sobering. I thought to myself, *It all ends as sure as it begins*. We come and we go and while it seems like we are here forever, forever is a perspective reserved for the young. Emmeline has forever. I have around thirty years.

Again, this all may sound cryptic, but our aversion to thinking about death is also an aversion to accepting the truth. Victims hide their eyes because the world is too scary. But heroes don't look away. They face the facts of reality and attempt to live an inspiring story within those facts.

Another truth is that death is not bad. All good stories have a beginning, a middle, and an end. And it is only because they end that they can be understood. When we are done living our stories is when a moral can be determined. Inspiration can be felt. Your story can live on in the memories of others and serve as a model for them to experience meaning.

Even as I grieve the fact this life with Betsy and Emmeline and even Lucy won't last forever, I reflect on the idea that death also serves us in many ways. Because we know that our stories will end, we are gifted a sense of urgency. If our stories went on forever, no action would be important because everything could wait till tomorrow. It's the sense of pending death that encourages us to get busy living.

Whether our stories are meaningful to ourselves or inspirational to others is entirely up to us.

Screenwriters and novelists often begin with the end of a story in mind before they start writing. It's an old writing strategy. You start with a final scene that is beautiful and meaningful and then reverse engineer the story to get to that scene.

I bring up all this talk of life and death because the best way to ensure our stories are filled with meaning is to perform a creative exercise: pretend we are at the end of our lives, look back, and write down what happened.

WRITE YOUR OWN EULOGY

To create your life plan, we'll go through a series of exercises and assignments. Each exercise is designed to help you think through and complete the assignments. In all, the assignments will help you create a life plan you can review as a morning ritual and also give you a daily planner so that you stay on track.

The first assignment we will perform in creating our life plan is to write our eulogy. At first this may sound morbid, but I hope you find it to be centering and even inspirational.

The next few chapters will help you think through your life and then write a eulogy that will anchor you and help you own more agency in your life.

Writing my eulogy has created a filter that helps me make better decisions.

This morning I could have finished watching that terrific documentary I started last night, the one Ken Burns created about the life of Ernest Hemingway. Instead I chose to open up this book and continue writing. Why? Because morning after morning I'm reminded that by the end of my life, I want to have been a man of words—words that built worlds. I can't do that by watching a documentary about a guy who wrote books. I actually have to write them myself.

There are several more ways writing our eulogy and processing the reality of our own deaths can make our lives more interesting and more meaningful.

A TICKING CLOCK CREATES A SENSE OF URGENCY

Storytellers use the tool of expiring time to ramp up the drama. Without a ticking clock, a story gets boring. The next time you watch a love story, notice the story isn't a simple tale about a couple that fall in love. Instead, you'll notice the movie is about a man who has fallen in love with a woman, but the woman is planning on marrying the hero's older brother who is a jerk, only the woman doesn't know that her fiancé is a jerk. The wedding is to take place next Saturday at noon, and our hero has only six days to convince her she's making a mistake!

Now that's a story.

Why? Because the deadline of next Saturday at noon forces action.

This is true in nearly every story you read or any movie you watch. The bomb must be disarmed before a certain time. The treasure must be found before the bad guys get to it.

Even in sports, it's the ticking clock that forces the drama. Our team must score two more times before the clock hits zero or else they'll lose the championship.

Without an expiring clock, it's difficult to make a story compelling.

OUR EULOGY DEFINES OUR ROLE

When I think about the role I'll play in the life of my wife and child, the only definitive description I can come up with is that

I want to serve as a foundation. Betsy will bring the warmth and the windows. She will bring the joy because she always does. She also brings a stability in her capacity to disarm tension. She will bring the nourishment. Women are miraculous beings. But I will not be unimportant in this operation. I want to be a foundation. I want the people I love to be able to build their dreams on me, and I want to be a stable foundation on which those dreams can rise. I want to stay low and stay strong.

But having an ambition for my life is not enough. Without the clock loudly clicking down to death in the background, I'd not feel the urgency to take action on my ambition to be a good father.

Actress and director Bryce Dallas Howard, the daughter of Ron Howard, made a documentary recently about fathers. It's called *Dads*. Betsy and I watched it together the other night. Ron Howard, who had a terrific father, worked to leave a legacy for his own children. Even while he built a successful career, he was always there for his kids. When I talk about serving as a foundation for my family, I cling to the three things Ron Howard said he tried to provide for his children: love, security, and an example to follow. I included the fact I wanted to provide love, security, and an example to follow in my eulogy.

If I didn't read my eulogy every morning, I would quickly forget my desire to be a good father. If we don't remind ourselves of whom we want to be every day, distractions can steal our story. If I hadn't written my own eulogy and read through it several times each week, I'd forget that I want my daughter to be able to say I set her up to succeed in love, work, and life. I want her to marry somebody who loves her as I love her mother. I want my story to have a beginning, a middle, and an end that will inspire the stories of the people I leave behind.

Without my eulogy, I'd probably forget I have limited time to live my story. I'd likely get distracted and numb myself with pleasure rather than accept the challenges life offers.

I don't want to distract myself from the task at hand, and that task is life.

To be clear, I'm not overly excited about the idea of death. I really, really like this life. It is full of hidden treasures, and I want to keep searching for them.

This is, perhaps, the downside of living a life in which you experience meaning. You cling to it all the more because it means all the more to you.

And yet, the storytellers are right. Were it not for the reality of death and our willingness to openly process it as a fact, we'd likely not cling to life at all. We don't tend to cling to things until we realize they are going to be taken away.

Death is serving each of us, day after day. Again, the reality of death provides a ticking clock that clarifies our values and creates a sense of urgency.

HOW LONG DO YOU HAVE LEFT TO LIVE?

We've already established that stories with a ticking clock increase the sense of urgency for the hero. When it comes to your life story, you only need to know how much time is on one clock: How long do you have to live? It's a puzzling question. But it's the clock you must face to increase the narrative traction you experience in your life.

How much longer do you have to live? How much longer till the credits roll on your story?

Nobody knows when they will die, exactly, but if we do a couple calculations, we can make an educated guess. The average American lives to be 78.5 years old. If you've got good genes, give yourself another five years or so, but if folks in your family tend to die younger, take off about five years. And that's about how long you have left.

If you've already passed 78.5 and are feeling good, you are among the people who are upping the curve. I have every intention of joining you. You may even have twenty years left. Scientists are now saying that children being born today will live to be one hundred. My grandmother even lived to be ninety-six.

If you've beaten the odds, there's a chance you have saved your best chapters for the end of the story. Whether or not your story has a great third act is, of course, up to you.

Regardless, whether you have sixty years or six months, life invites you to live a great story with the time you have left.

I only press on this reality because I believe numbering our days benefits us. As I've already said, the stakes of a story are only heightened by the ticking of a countdown clock.

How much time do *you* have left?

Take a moment and reflect on how old you will be when you pass. If you are married, how old will your spouse be when you pass? If you have children, how old will they be when you pass?

EXERCISE QUESTION ONE:

I will likely pass away when I am about _____ years old.

EXERCISE QUESTION TWO:

If I die when I am _____ years old, that means I only have _____ years left to live.

For the rest of this book you can use the software or printout to create your life plan. Scan the QR code below to begin the journey.

8

. . . .

A Good Eulogy Talks About Who and What the Hero Loved

BETSY HAD ME TAKE a baby blanket home from the hospital the day before we brought Emmeline home. She'd read that if you bring home the scent of the baby and familiarize your dog, the dog will somehow know the person was safe. I'm not sure about all that, but I know when we brought Emmeline through the front gate, Lucy sensed immediately somebody special had come home. She crept down the steps and stood her stiff legs straight. Panting, her tail wagged behind her like a flag. We set the car seat down and Lucy sniffed around Emmeline's toes, looking up at us as though to affirm our accomplishment. Emmeline's tiny arms flung reflexively toward the sky. Lucy didn't have any questions. She'd protected the two of us for years. She could handle one more.

I know it sounds strange to say it, but I hope that one day Emmeline has a dog as loyal as Lucy. And I hope she has friends as excited to see her. As I rock my daughter to sleep, my number one prayer for her is that she will have the wisdom to choose good friends and the ambition to create community. I ask God to give Emmeline kind, gracious, and wise people to be with, all her life.

A good story isn't just about the hero. It's about the people the hero loves, the people dependent on the hero, the victim the hero is going to rescue. Stories may be told through the lens of the hero, but they are almost always about what is happening to a community of people.

The next exercise we will do in preparation of writing our eulogy is to consider who we are living our stories with and who we are living our stories for.

After defining a project to work on or a mission to join, the next necessary element of a meaningful life, according to Viktor Frankl, involves the community we belong to and a general awareness of what's going on outside ourselves.

In stories, heroes are determined to complete their tasks with and on behalf of others.

It's a characteristic of heroes that their ambitions are not entirely selfish. Certainly they're going to get some glory for their accomplishment, but the fact that their actions are benefiting the lives of others makes their actions more meaningful.

Often, screenwriters go through enormous pains to show the hero's relational connections. We meet the hero's mother and her father, her sister, her friends, her kids. We sit and watch them have deep conversations with their loved ones, working through conflicts. And why? Because we root for people who connect deeply with others, and we are suspicious of those who do not.

When our lives consider the welfare of others, our stories improve.

Villains stand in contrast to heroes in this regard. Villains do not have friends, they have minions. Villains surround themselves with people who do their bidding out of fear. To the villain, people are expendable. They do not love people; they use people. Villains may look like they have friends, but they do not. Friends forgive each other and work through problems. Villains dispose of their minions when they no longer find them useful.

Without question, people are drawn to villains, but not because they sense in them a companion. What people are drawn to is protection.

In fact, confusing strength for security is why people become a villain's minion. When we perceive ourselves as weak and in need of a strong person to protect us, we are more likely to submit to a villain and serve them in order to associate with that strength. Minions believe if they are loyal to the villain, the villain will be loyal to them. This is almost never the case. Again, villains do not intimately connect with others. Villains use others.

In Disney's origin story of Cruella de Vil, the screenwriters tell the terrifically imagined story of Estella, an orphaned girl who, upon encountering a villainous fashion baron, attempts to destroy her empire by disrupting the market with beautiful designs of her own.

It must have been difficult to tell the story of a historic villain and yet have an audience sympathize and even root for her. But the storytellers navigated the terrain well. The first trick was to create an even worse villain so that Cruella's crimes didn't look all that bad. Second was to surround her with sympathetic friends. Her makeshift orphan family included Jasper and Horace along with their pet dog, Wink.

What is interesting about the story is that when the character reveals her heroic instincts, she is Estella and treats Jasper and Horace as equals, even brothers. But when she surfaces her villainous instincts as Cruella, she treats her former friends as cogs in a machine that generates vengeance. She treats them as though they are her minions.

If taken too far, the audience would have turned on Cruella. But in an attempt to lure the audience back to her side, she repents for her mistreatment and reconciles with her friends, all before the final scene.

In other words, the characteristic the screenwriters chose to differentiate Cruella from Estella, the hero from the villain, was how she treated her friends. I think that's a life lesson for us.

This vacillation between villain and hero is common among the powerful. As their responsibilities increase and they find themselves working with an ever-larger team, the temptation to use others rather than work with them increases. Many a celebrity has been taken down by former friends who had suddenly been reduced to minions.

The kinds of relationships we have in our lives matter. We may be tempted to use others rather than connect with them, but those actions will cost us. While many scenarios make a chain of command necessary, heroes and guides genuinely care about the people they work with.

As you write your eulogy, you'll want to consider the friends and family you will leave behind.

But what do you do if you don't have a rich community from which to live your story?

Another factor to consider as you write your eulogy is the community you create.

If you think about it, relationships and community are baked into the fabric of life by design. Even the birth of Emmeline is a designed plot twist to force Betsy and me into an intense relational exchange with each other and the baby.

What could be more disruptive than a child? Suddenly life is not so much about what we want as it is about keeping a vulnerable and helpless being alive.

Remember, Viktor Frankl prescribed community to his patients in order for them to experience meaning. When we live with and amongst others in some way we create more opportunities to experience the logotherapy that generates meaning.

No doubt, relationships are hard. But when something is hard, it invites focus and intensity. Children are perhaps the most powerful element in life to pull us out of ourselves.

As I talked with other parents about what to expect when the baby comes, their descriptions were justifiably confusing. They talked about an explosion of love, but also explosions of poop.

In fact, in the weeks since we have become parents, the best synopsis I can give about parenthood is that it is like drowning in love. The night shifts and lack of sleep, the inconsolable crying and the fear she isn't getting enough food, or the room is too cold, or she's not breathing quite right drive a kind of paranoia that is exacerbated when combined with sleep deprivation. Yet you somehow love the process, and the harder it gets, the more you're committed to the cause. Having a child is a myriad of contrasting emotions. It's like Betsy and I have found ourselves floating down the rapids of love, having our heads bashed violently against the rocks of joy and fulfillment.

I confess that even before we became parents, other parents sounded a little bit like addicts. They stood there holding their cute little drug in their arms, beckoning us to join them. Their eyes were red, their hair disheveled, their smiles wide.

It's true, Emmeline has made us addicts like them. Happy, exhausted, moody, and temperamental addicts.

And yet, it's all by design. Relationships, especially intimate and difficult ones, contribute to the quality of our stories and to the deep sense of meaning we are after.

When we write our eulogy, it would be easy just to think about our accomplishments or our projects without including the many people who touched our lives or whose lives we have impacted.

Remembering our spouse, our children, our friends, and our coworkers gives our eulogy a depth of meaning. It also reminds us, while we are performing our morning ritual, that relationships matter.

Again, the second element of Viktor Frankl's logotherapy is to "encounter something or someone" and, again, by this he means to share our life's focus with something or someone outside ourselves. We can't do this if we are playing the villain or the victim.

In fact, you could make a good argument that one of the problems with victim mindset is that victims only think of themselves. Of course, actual victims have every reason to: they are imprisoned with no way out. But our tendency to see ourselves as victims when in fact we are not drains meaning from our lives by not allowing us to connect in healthy relationships.

Healthy connection happens when two people enter into a mutually beneficial relationship. When you have something that makes me happy and I have something that makes you happy and we exchange those things, the relationship flourishes. But when we play the victim, we find ourselves taking more than we give.

You've likely experienced a dynamic called Karpman's drama triangle. Stephen Karpman is a psychiatrist who explained what happens when we interact with somebody who sees themselves as a victim even though they are not. The first stage is when the person positions themselves as a victim in order to attract a rescuer. Then, the rescuer swoops in to make themselves feel good by helping a victim. Then, when the rescuer's resources and patience wear thin, they begin to blame and persecute the very person they were attempting to rescue.

If you look back on your life, you likely see yourself having played all three of those roles. Regardless, entering into Karpman's triangle makes a healthy relationship difficult, if not impossible.

Again, healthy relationships exist between people who find each other mutually beneficial. They are each strong in their own right, giving to the other out of their strength and generosity.

I once wrote in a book that true love doesn't keep score. I admit now I was wrong. It's not that we should all go around scorekeeping, but it's true that in healthy relationships, you want to give as much as you take because giving and receiving create a virtuous cycle that builds intimacy.

Regardless, relationships are a critical part of a meaningful story. Without them, and without tending to them, it will be difficult to discover a life of meaning.

A HERO ON A MISSION NOTICES THE WORLD

But "other people" is not the only way Frankl says we can experience life outside ourselves. Nature, in all its beauty, turns our minds away from ourselves and draws us into the world around us. Not only nature, but art, both its creation and appreciation, can help us get out of our heads. Good food. Good music. Stories we love. These are all ways to engage and appreciate "the other."

A memory I cherish from my single years is the season I spent on Orcas Island in the San Juans. I went there to finish a book. It was winter; no tourists were there. Few people live on the island year-round, so I found myself mostly alone. My time was split between writing my book, kayaking around the island, and getting up early with Lucy to climb the hills and capture sunrise with my camera. While I was certainly lonely, there was something about intentionally getting out into nature that eased the pain. The world was bigger than me, bigger than my problems.

Even Lucy has helped me get out of my own head.

Well into my thirties, unmarried and lonely, it was that chocolate Lab that helped me find some sanity and wellness. Just having a creature that needed me to be home, needed to go on walks, needed to play, and needed to nap provided constant reminders that the world was not only about me. Lucy helped me learn that I am an interdependent part of a larger, living organism.

By saying we need to become interested in other people and things outside ourselves, I believe Frankl is telling us to find something in life we love—something that strikes a sense of awe inside us—and then make it a daily habit to engage whatever that is. "The other" can distract us from our mild narcissistic tendencies.

Reading my eulogy reminds me that engaging with other people and other things is important.

It's in reading my eulogy that I remember I am not only here to build a business, but to share life with others, to appreciate art and music and food, and to build a community.

COULD YOU CREATE A COMMUNITY?

Often, people aren't satisfied with their community. They feel alone or they just don't click with the people around them. Again, though, when we feel alone we are tempted to see ourselves as a victim, as though fate has determined we are to be alone. But this isn't true.

One of the things I admire most in people is the ability to create community. As I said, the ambition to create community is the number one prayer I pray for my daughter. I'm not talking about joining a community, though that is fine. I'm talking about the art of actually creating whatever kind of community you want.

Why trust fate to dictate what your social life looks like? Why not create the community of your dreams?

When I was a bachelor, I'd open my home to musicians traveling through Portland. And even though I lived in the Pacific Northwest, I ended up with an amazing community of musicians, most of whom lived in Nashville. Within a few years, I was entertaining fifty or more overnight guests each year, most of them on tour. It was a fun season.

When Betsy and I moved to Nashville, we had a built-in community of people we cared about and who cared about us. Just opening up my home to singer/songwriters on tour created a community I still love today.

You can create a community for any reason at any time. You don't have to ask permission.

Want to create a community around your backyard garden? Just find a few families, offer them a little plot, and choose a time to plant tomatoes together.

I recommend making the community about something other than just sitting around and talking. Find an excuse to bring people together and they will come. Some of the ideas Betsy and I have come up with are hosting a poetry night or showing a movie in our backyard. When Betsy and I first moved to Nashville, we invited guest speakers to come and talk about the Israeli/Palestinian conflict. No kidding, without even knowing him, I invited the governor to attend because the governor's mansion was in the neighborhood next door. He showed! He literally walked right in the door and sat and listened to the lecture. How cool is that?

Later, we hosted a local politician to answer questions about issues that affected our congressional district. We've hosted cocktail classes and cooking classes. We've hosted book releases and birthday parties. It hardly matters. Just bring people together to do something and the magic will happen.

COMMUNITY WILL FEED YOUR SOUL

Creating a community can happen the second we realize we have the agency to do so.

A couple years ago I met a woman named Sarah Harmeyer who started a company called Neighbor's Table. After years of chasing professional success, she realized having a lot of money and power wasn't going to fulfill her. What made her happy was sitting around a table and sharing a meal with friends.

She also realized she didn't know her neighbors. She looked around at the houses within a hundred yards of her home and realized she didn't know the stories of the people who lived closest to her.

She asked her father to make a table so she could invite her neighbors over for a meal. Her father, Lee, relished the opportunity. He'd recently retired and was looking for something to do. Once Lee delivered the table, Sarah started cooking. That year she invited more than five hundred friends and neighbors to dinner. She says it was one of the most meaningful years of her life.

Wanting to share the joy, Lee and Sarah started Neighbor's Table. They make, sell, and deliver tables all over the country to people who make a commitment to get to know their neighbors.

"Some people think I'm in the table business," Sarah says. "But I'm in the people business."

Today, Neighbor's Table has handcrafted and delivered more than five hundred tables.

Creating an intentional community does take time, but the investment pays.

Taking a cue from Sarah, I decided to create yet another community that was missing in my life.

A couple years ago I realized that as the CEO of a small company, I felt alone. There weren't many people I could talk to about the challenges of growing a business.

I decided to start a community called "The Advisory Board." Basically, it's a group of new friends who run similar-size companies. We meet twice each year to have some fun and share conversations about our unique challenges.

We usually get together in nature. Betsy let me know before we were married that she "does not camp." So my friends and I either rent a house on a beachside cliff or take motorcycles and ATVs into the wilderness. We go out in search of wonder and awe so we can be more grounded in meaning when we return to our lives.

It's out in the wilderness, sitting around a fire, where my soul finds food. Sharing my concerns with the other members of the advisory board and knowing we aren't alone in our challenges allows me to come home stronger.

Heroes on a mission attract heroes on a mission. I want to do life with people who hunt meaning and share the hunt with their friends.

And again, it's not just people that we need in our lives. It's art and nature. Betsy and I take regular walks with Emmeline out at Radnor Lake, counting the turtles we see sunbathing on the logs. I wonder if Emmeline will learn to count by helping us count turtles.

Not only this, but my friend Nita Andrews and I are working to curate a book called *Poems for Children to Memorize* in which we will print fifty or more poems children (and parents) should memorize before the kids are seventeen. If Emmeline is up for it, I'll be paying her a reward fee for every poem she memorizes. I'm hoping the experiment costs me a great deal of money, and also helps her spend countless hours thinking about beautiful things in the world (and for that matter not thinking about ugly things in the world).

As we continue to consider what our eulogy will say, we need to pause for a moment and take an honest assessment of our experience of the other. Have we created a community, or are we simply trusting fate with the all-important nurturing we need?

Are we taking time off to appreciate the natural world around us?

Are we pausing to reflect on the art and music that serves to memorialize our collective human experience?

Let's not hope a community happens to us. Let's build one. And let's not forget to involve ourselves in the arts and in nature. You will find, even though it may cost you some productivity, that being aware of the beauty around you will contribute to a deep sense of meaning.

To answer these reflection questions, list the names of people you want to invite into a community and the ways in which you will engage the natural and artistic worlds outside yourself.

EXERCISE QUESTION THREE:

Where will you find community? What will you create or join that will embed you in a community of people you care about and who care about you?

What communities will you join or start?

_____

_____

_____

_____

EXERCISE QUESTION FOUR:

How will you choose to engage nature or art and help yourself become more aware of the world outside yourself?

Where will you go and what will you do to experience more nature and art?

_____

_____

_____

_____

By writing about the community we will create or join, and by listing the ways we will appreciate nature and art, we are reminding ourselves, over and over, that life is not about us. It's about sharing our human experience with other people.

A HERO SHARES AGENCY WITH OTHER CHARACTERS

As we begin to share our lives with others, we will surface all new challenges. Including others in your life, your vision, and your story isn't easy. When others are involved, we have to make compromises. Our story becomes less about an individual hero and more about a group of protagonists seeking meaning.

Before Betsy and I were married, neither of us would have dreamed of living on fifteen acres and running what amounts to an informal retreat center. Betsy would rather live in the French Quarter of New Orleans, or perhaps Manhattan or Paris. She wanted to be able to walk to a bakery. She wanted to share life with friends who lived next door. She did not want to build a business or, as previously disclosed, lie under the trees in a camping tent. *There are no ticks dropping from the ceiling of a bakery,* she reminds me.

I, on the other hand, would want to live on an island, preferably in a cabin with a wood-burning stove and a boat tied to a buoy just off the shore of a deep, dark sound. Lucy and I would sail around the San Juans, docking only to eat or attend a concert or a Seahawks game, often forgetting where exactly our cabin was so that we'd have to find our way home by the light of the moon.

With Betsy, though, I do not live the story I want to live, and she does not live the story she wants to live. We have sacrificed those stories. We now live the story *we* want to live. The two of us have become something other, something with dreams of its own, and they are wonderful dreams. While I like the idea of my dreams, I prefer the dreams that happen when Betsy and I connect our stories. I would not trade the front porch I share with Betsy for a sailboat on the sound. I would not trade the view of her picking flowers in the garden for the moon rolling over the water. We have both compromised and discovered the story of *we* is better than the story of *me*.

That said, I still camp with my friends. And Betsy still visits big cities and eats at bakeries.

I wonder how Emmeline will change our story. I can't wait to find out.

Again, the idea that we must share life, that we must find something that draws our attention outside ourselves, is an element neccessary to create a life of meaning. According to Frankl, if we find something or someone outside ourselves that reduces our inward focus, we will begin to experience even more narrative traction. We will become more interested in our own lives. For me, that used to be the rivers and the mountains. Now, it is more friends and family. Regardless, it's *the other* that contributes to the sense of meaning we get to experience every day.

Who or what draws you out of yourself?

In your eulogy, talk about what you listed in exercise three and four; talk about your appreciation for the world and for the people around you.

But it's not time to write your eulogy just yet. A good story needs more than an ambition, a community, and an appreciation for nature and art. It also needs a vision that requires risk.

9

. . . .

A Good Eulogy Helps You
Find Narrative Traction

NOW THAT WE KNOW we need to include other people in our lives and/or find a way to appreciate art and nature, what are we going to do? What kind of story can we live that will require us to expand our scope so that others are involved? It's time to start dreaming up a new story.

There is yet another factor that is necessary to make our eulogy interesting (and to find meaning in the actual living of that eulogy). We need to create something new; we need to bring a reality into the world that did not previously exist. And to do this we will have to accept our own agency to effect change.

The ultimate sign that we have accepted our own agency is when we see ourselves as creators, not just consumers.

Consumers buy things other people create and either like those things or complain about those things. Creators, on the other hand, actually create the things consumers consume. I'm not just talking about products here, but stories and adventures and real-life experiences.

Creators make things that did not previously exist. They make companies and paintings and songs. They even make other people. If there is one unique characteristic that sets the human animal apart from other species, it's that a human can envision a different world and then work to create it.

When I talk about creating something, I'm not just talking about creating something grand and impressive. Even though there are people who build rocket ships and go to space or win Olympic medals, the meaning we get from creating something epic and creating something simple is the same.

In fact, the most meaning I've ever created in life came from the birth of our daughter. As a guy who chases meaning, this was surprising to me. I thought meaning required enormous risk and grandiose plans, but it doesn't. It simply requires dreaming up something that doesn't exist and doing the work to make it exist.

Emmeline is, of course, not a project. And technically God made her. But when we brought her into the world, we created a new kind of marriage and a new kind of home and a new way of seeing the world. As my mother-in-law said to us when the baby was born, "Remember, Emmeline isn't a problem to fix, she's a relationship to build."

Building a new relationship is a beautiful act of creation.

With Emmeline, I want to create a relationship in which I am a good dad. A fun dad. A creative dad. A present dad. A forgiving dad. A wise dad. These things can happen, but only if I do the work to make them happen.

There are times when I find myself wondering if Emmeline and I will have a strong relationship. Certainly things can go wrong. I don't get to control how Emmeline feels about me. But whether or not I'm the kind of person she wants a relationship with is actually entirely up to me. And that's an awful big part of the equation.

This is another reason victimhood is a sad state. The psychologist Alfred Adler taught that when we see ourselves as inferior, as victims who are not wanted or needed, we are intentionally choosing that view to protect ourselves from the possibility of getting hurt in relationships. He argued that we should stop seeing ourselves as victims and have the courage to take chances in interpersonal relationships, boldly and humbly putting ourselves out there in order to create the intimacy we need in life.

There has been a lot of pushback to Adler's theories stating that many people have trauma that causes them to be fearful in relationships. This is determinism. Adler acknowledges trauma affects us, but believed it affects us only because it offers a greater excuse to retreat into victim mentality and shield ourselves from further damage. The choice to retreat, he argues, is ours. We are not determined by our past trauma. He believed we do not have to be controlled by the outside forces of past experiences as the past no longer exists.

Adler's ideas will be debated for centuries to come, of course, and while I believe we are certainly affected by trauma, I do not believe trauma has to dictate our futures at all. Two people may experience the same trauma but their responses to that trauma will determine their futures. The trauma does not have power; the person who experiences the trauma has power. I believe Adler's ideas are helpful in the sense that they return agency to the victim, encouraging the victim to see their pain as a choice they are continuing to make—thus giving the victim power over their pain and helping them transition into a heroic mindset regarding their circumstances. After all, if our pain and fear comes from past trauma, past trauma controls our lives and our agency remains external.

It does make you wonder if some of our victim tendencies aren't self-chosen.

Regardless, it is difficult for people who self-identify as victims to connect, as when we see ourselves as victims we have a hard time believing we are worth connecting with.

Freud may have said "trauma has made you a victim" while Adler would say "trauma has given you an excuse to see yourself as a victim and because you fear relationships, being a victim gives you an excuse not to connect."

Villains have an even harder time creating relationships. Of course, they believe they can change the world, but they use their agency to create a world in which others are weak so that the villains themselves can feel powerful. They seek vengeance. They seek power as a show of strength to fend off foes. Again, they use people rather than connect with people. In order to accomplish their perverted vision, they railroad others into submission. A vision like this, though, does not produce a deep experience of meaning because we cannot control people and love them at the same time. To love people we must set them free to decide on their own accord whether they want to love us back. Villains do not take these kinds of relational risks. They are too afraid people won't be loyal to them, so they control those they are close to and use them to bring about a feeling of self-protection.

Heroes and guides contend with villains by bringing more light than darkness into the world. If heroes make the world better than villains make it worse, then the world improves. But the more heroes slip into the deception that they are actually victims, surrendering their agency to others or to fate, the more ground villains will take.

Regardless of whether we want to create community, intimacy, art, a product, a company, a book, a nonprofit, or anything else, we will have to accept our agency to do so. Nothing will change until we decide to bring something new into the world and trust in our God-given abilities.

So, that being said, what should we want? What are the characteristics of a vision that helps us experience a deep sense of meaning?

There is another truth in story that is applicable to life: the hero should want something specific.

Too many of us want *more personal freedom* or *more time with our kids* or to somehow *be heard and understood*. While those things are noble, they aren't specific enough to generate narrative traction.

If I invited you to skip work and go with me to a movie about a "guy looking for fulfillment," you'd likely turn me down. A movie about a "guy looking for fulfillment" doesn't sound that interesting. It's not clear what the movie is really about.

If I invited you to skip work because another one of Liam Neeson's daughters had been kidnapped and we could watch him get her back at a matinee, you'd be more likely to attend. When the hero wants something specific, something the audience can actually picture in their minds, the audience is more likely to experience narrative traction and stick with the story through to its end.

In order to invite ourselves into a story, then, the vision we have for our lives must also be clear and specific. It will not do to say I have a vision of being a "good person" or of "building a community." These vague assertions will die on our lips. Instead, we will build a grocery store in which the homeless population of our town can shop for free. Nashville locals Brad and Kim Paisley did exactly that and no doubt experienced a deep sense of meaning as they hatched their exciting plan and sacrificed to make it happen.

Again, a specific vision isn't necessarily a grandiose vision. We can invite ten close friends to a golfing retreat in which we create our life plans together. We can work with the kids to build a garden and sell tomatoes at the local farmers market, or for that matter on the sidewalk in front of our home. We can start a father/son community of friends who go fishing every year in Montana. We can start a mother/daughter community to teach young women about politics and show them what it would look like to run for office someday. We can create a bunch of enormous bingo boards, buy binoculars, and identify two hundred species of birds in our region. The list of things we can do with our lives is immense.

After the murder of George Floyd I looked around and realized I had built a mostly white company. The business had grown so big so fast, I'd neglected to make it diverse. I confessed I'd been operating with a subconscious bias. Still, I didn't just want to send out an Instagram quote and pretend I cared about the issue. Instead, I started a Black-owned business cohort so I could get to know the Black entrepreneurial community in Nashville and grow our team through friendships and understanding. To say the least, the experience has been eye opening.

Again, we may want things like fulfillment and joy and equality and love, but to get those things we have to enter into specific stories.

Definitive, specific plans tend to get accomplished while vague assertions wisp weakly into the wind. Why? Because vague and elusive notions do not help us find narrative traction. When we are vague, we have trouble getting our minds around the story question that invites us into our own lives. A story question such as "Will I expand my understanding of the arts?" does not create the kind of narrative traction of "Will I memorize twenty-five poems and be able to recite any of them at any given time?"

The first story question is vague while the second is specific. The first story question does not generate narrative traction while the second story question does.

It's also okay to have several story questions going at once. Stories, after all, have plots and subplots that work together to weave into a fantastic overall tale. If your subplots all fit under your main plot, you won't get too jumbled with so many ambitions.

Right now, Betsy and I have a few stories brewing. We've got narrative traction (meaning we're invested and contributing to the resolution) of the build-out of Goose Hill and are using it to positively impact the world. That story, by the way, is certainly about making the world a better place, but it's much more about doing something fun, hard, and meaningful with our family. Emmeline will grow up thinking it's normal to grow a garden so guests can eat the tomatoes, and she'll think it's normal to attend a pop-up art gallery in the backyard. And why shouldn't such things be normal? They can be, so why not make it so?

Many people will read this book and say my story is easier because I've succeeded financially. That's true, but it's also true I only succeeded financially because I wrote down a vision to start a company and then did so. Victims believe other people can do things that they cannot do. As Alfred Adler taught, we have to be careful we aren't generating a victim mindset in an effort to protect ourselves from trying, or, perhaps, protect ourselves from the frustration and self-doubt involved in attempting to master something new. Besides, it does not take money to experience a deep sense of meaning. It takes vision. All we have to do is make one vision happen and then dream up another. What you'll find is the compound interest on living terrific stories adds up fast.

Again, the point here is to make the visions you have for your health and your career and your community and your family specific. The more specific they are, the more narrative traction you'll create and the more excited you'll be to wake up in the morning and put a little something on the plot.

What is the vision you have for your life? What will the "things you did" be when your friends and family sit at your funeral and read your eulogy?

When it's done, your eulogy will read like a summary of the story of your life. And even though you won't be there to hear it, you get to have been the person to live it. Every day, we write a page that people will someday read. Not only this, but how grateful will your friends and family be because you involved them in so many of those stories? And how grateful will they be knowing that because you lived such remarkable stories, you inspired them to do the same?

BUT HOW DO WE KNOW WHAT TO WANT?

Occasionally I'll meet somebody who doesn't quite know what they want. They know they want to enjoy life, but they aren't sure how to go about it. What kinds of things should we want? What makes for a good ambition in our stories?

In order to help you find narrative traction, here are three characteristics of a good ambition.

1. The vision should probably embarrass you.

It's okay to be a little embarrassed when you share what you want to do with your life. Being a little embarrassed means you want to do something that other people might not think you are able to do. Or worse, you want to do something that threatens your community's status quo. But remember, we are all people who can transform into better versions of ourselves.

To be sure, striving for a creative ambition will invite push-back. People want you to stay in your lane and not threaten the tribal pecking order. But here's a secret I learned years ago: after the initial power tussle, usually consisting of a few passive-aggressive comments, everybody accepts the new pecking order. To experience a great life and accomplish much, you just have to be willing to make a few people uncomfortable for a few minutes. Or maybe a few months.

Your friends and family will get used to you and your ambitions. As I said earlier, it's true that other drivers often honk when you change lanes. Let them. They'll stop after a minute and then you'll get more comfortable in the new lane, the one that takes you to better and better places.

Who are you to want something so big? But then who is anybody? Aren't you anybody? Aren't you somebody? Aren't you a walking miracle of flesh and skin and voice? You didn't make you. God made you. Maybe He made you to live a story, not just watch other people live stories from deep in the cheap seats.

If we want to live a meaningful story, we can't hide.

Just last night a friend in my small business group pulled me aside after our meeting. We'd all gone around and read our eulogies to one another, each of us significantly moved by the visions we'd laid out for our lives. But Shanera did not read hers, and after the meeting she told me why. The truth is, she wanted to write a book. She wanted to show the world the beauty and challenge of being a Black mother raising Black children in a white upper-class neighborhood. She wanted her friends to know how often her teenage children get pulled over by police. She wanted the people she loved to hear about life in their community but from a different perspective. She wanted to expand her friends' understanding of the world so that it was more true, more relevant. She was going to call the book *Brown Mamma Bear.* Listening to her, I was moved. *Shanera, there's a story there,* I said. *The world needs that book right now.* She looked at me, puzzled. She seemed to be saying, "Who am I to tell my story?" But in our current cultural climate, don't you agree it is imperative she offers the world her perspective? Her story would be good medicine for all of us. It would heal some of the cuts we've made in others and stop us from cutting further. And it would help other women like Shanera know they are not alone.

We cannot let a little *who am I to do X?* stop us from living an exciting story that inspires the people around us.

If the vision you have for your life embarrasses you a little bit and makes you wonder if people are going to say, "Who do you think you are to want X?" then you're on to a story that will gain you a little narrative traction and contribute to your sense of meaning.

2. The vision should probably scare you.

On my team, we have a saying: "Swim out past the breakers." By that we mean to make sure you are stretching yourself as a professional. We love throwing people into publicity campaigns even though they have no experience as a publicist. We love handing our design team software ideas that they aren't quite sure they can pull off.

Why do the members of my team need to swim out past the breakers? Because I firmly believe a learning and development company should develop their people. And the only way we learn is to fumble at a skill we've yet to master until we get it right.

Swimming out past the breakers means we are just out past the waves where our feet hardly touch the bottom. Every once in a while we feel sand on our toes, but most of the time we are floating—and a little worried we're getting sucked out to sea.

Building a home, starting a business, giving a speech, or running for office are terrifying prospects, but they are only terrifying because we've yet to stretch ourselves.

There is no other way for a character to transform except to try to do things they didn't know they were capable of doing.

3. It must be realistic.

Now that I've convinced you to jump off a cliff, stop.

Our stories must also be realistic so that we can actually, or at least likely, bring our vision into the real world.

If you want to be a famous country singer but you do not know how to play the guitar, write songs, or sing, you are not likely to succeed. If you are fifty-seven and want to play quarterback in the NFL, it won't happen.

There is a difference between swimming out past the breakers and putting a sandwich in a Ziploc bag, tucking it into the waistband of your bathing suit, and swimming toward China.

Do not think reading this book will make your dreams come true. It won't. This is not a book of chants you can recite to force the genie out of the lamp and grant you three wishes (although those books seem to sell well).

Can the vision you have established for your life actually happen? Are other people who have your basic skill set doing what you want to do? If so, good. If somebody else like you is doing it, you can probably do it yourself. And if nobody is doing it, don't let that stop you if the vision is actually attainable. Be the first.

Is there a big vision you want to accomplish before you die? If so, what is it? And if there is more than one, reflect on each and write them down so you can include them in your eulogy. I've broken down your vision brainstorm into separate categories in hopes it will help. You don't have to have a vision for each, though. Simply come up with a few specific ambitions you'd like to bring about in life and you'll be on your way.

EXERCISE FIVE:

Finish the following statements.

Something I'd like to create to experience better community is:

Something I'd like to create to unite my family is:

Something I'd like to do that will cause me to become healthier is:

Something I'd like to do to enhance my career is:

Something I'd like to do to develop myself intellectually is:

Something I'd like to do to expand my understanding of humanity is:

To print out the exercises and assignments that help you create your life plan, or to use the online daily planner software, scan the QR code below.

10

. . . .

Write Your Eulogy

NOW THAT WE HAVE reflected on how long we have left to live, what we want to do on earth, and who we want to share our lives with, it's time to imagine what kind of story we want to live.

The first assignment in the Hero on a Mission Life Plan is to write your eulogy.

Writing your eulogy and then reviewing it in your morning ritual will benefit you in four ways:

1. **Create a filter:** Because your eulogy will include at least one major project you've worked on, it will provide a vision for your life. That vision will create a filter helping you decide how to spend your time. Having a project that requires you to take action will help you experience a deep sense of meaning.
2. **Create community:** Because your eulogy will mention the people you live your story with and for, it will remind you to remain connected to the people you love. Being rela-

tionally connected is one of the elements that help you experience a deep sense of meaning.

3. **Redeem your challenges:** Knowing that the challenges you face each day will contribute to a better world gives purpose and meaning to the conflict you encounter. The challenges you encounter are transforming you into a more healthy, better version of yourself. This perspective will contribute to a deeper experience of meaning.

4. **Generate narrative traction:** Reviewing your life plan will actually help you accomplish your vision by creating cognitive dissonance. When you compare what your life is supposed to be like to the way your life is now, your mind will generate a kind of tension. This cognitive dissonance will motivate behaviors that ease the tension. The only way to alleviate the cognitive dissonance is to actually become the person you are reading about.

YOUR EULOGY WILL EVOLVE OVER TIME

Consider the first pass of your eulogy a rough draft. Your life plan is designed to be edited; it should evolve over time. Let's not consider our life plan a fixed document we must obey. I review my eulogy and change it a few times each year even though I wrote it for the first time nearly ten years ago. Remember, this isn't your actual eulogy; it's a creative tool that will help you build narrative traction in your life and also help you make better decisions.

But before you write your eulogy, here are some suggestions you will find helpful:

• *Keep it short.* You will be tempted to get long-winded, but remember you'll be reading this as part of your morning ritual. If it's too long, you'll find yourself skipping this reflection and moving straight into filling out the planner. I do that myself sometimes, but I try not to do it too frequently. Your eulogy will serve as a North Star. Take your eye off it and you're more likely to wander off the path. Keep it short so it's more likely to do the job you need it to do: help you create narrative traction.

- *Make it ambitious but realistic.* If you're fifty and hope to win Olympic gold on the Serbian rugby team, your eulogy is not going to help you create narrative traction because it will find nothing but dead ends in the actual living. The vision you have for your life must be ambitious enough to posit a story question (will you get it done?) without being so delusional that it's simply impossible. That said, I never thought I'd actually become a bestselling author or run a company or marry a woman as incredible as Betsy. You're likely able to accomplish more than you think, so make the vision you have for your life ambitious. Also, remember, it doesn't matter whether the vision actually comes true. Meaning is found by taking action toward a vision, not by accomplishing that vision. Whether you accomplish what you want or not, you'll find meaning in the attempt.
- *Don't get bogged down in the details.* Stating the date you'll die and listing the people you are survived by is the stuff of a real eulogy. But this isn't a real eulogy. This exercise is about creating a vision for your life that you find compelling. It isn't about anything else. This is a fictional document you are going to live into so that it's more likely to become true. Again, the point is narrative traction.

You don't have to include everything. There are plenty of projects and communities I'm working on in my life that are not listed in my eulogy. These things may show up in my ten-, five-, or one-year vision, but they aren't necessary in my eulogy. The point of the eulogy is "general direction" when it comes to my story. We've made space to include more projects in the vision worksheets and the goal-setting worksheets that we will explore later in this book.

Not sure what all to include in your eulogy? Here is a brief checklist of things you can include to make it interesting enough to inspire the narrative traction you will need to move into a meaningful life experience:

- What major projects did you work on and accomplish?
- Why did you choose those projects? What message were you trying to send to the world?
- What causes were you passionate about and how did you defend them?
- What significant relationships did you engage in and what do those people mean to you?
- What communities did you belong to or create?
- What is the legacy you hope to leave behind?
- How did you want people to feel about themselves after they interacted with you?
- What significant challenges did you overcome?
- What's the one thing you want others to remember you for?
- What one piece of wisdom do you want to pass along to those who come behind you?

Of course you don't need to include all of these elements. Your eulogy is your eulogy. All you need to do is write a paragraph or two that inspires you enough that you want to wake up in the morning and put a little something on the plot.

WHEN AND WHERE TO WRITE YOUR EULOGY

If you want to take a crack at writing your eulogy right now, feel free. Consider that attempt a rough draft. The actual assignment should be a little more reflective. When HOAM is taught in a workshop or class, the assignment of writing your eulogy is given a full hour so that participants have time to reflect. And again, don't forget that it's an evolving document. There will be times you'll think of something you want to do with your life while you're on a walk or taking a shower. Edit and develop your eulogy over time.

Many people who create the Hero on a Mission Life Plan set aside a morning or even go on a weekend retreat to make sure they have enough time to reflect. You want to think of your eulogy and life plan as an outline for a novel. The more time you spend on your outline, the easier it will be to write the book.

The same is true for this process: the more time you spend on your life plan, the easier it will be to live an interesting story and experience a deep sense of meaning.

What does a working HOAM eulogy look like? Here are a few samples, starting with my own:

DONALD MILLER

Donald Miller was a loving husband to his wife, Betsy, and an ever-present father to their daughter, Emmeline. His number one priority in life was always his family, which is why he limited his travel and work schedule to enjoy time with the people he loved the most.

Don and his family built a home called Goose Hill in which many friends, family members, and invited guests found rest and encouragement. Don, Betsy, and Emmeline loved to practice hospitality and were always surrounded by people who were working to make the world better.

Goose Hill housed book readings, picnics, small concerts, fundraisers, planning sessions for bipartisan political initiatives, family game nights, lectures, poetry groups, and many other activities that helped people get some rest, gave them hope, and cast a light on important ideas being brought into the world.

The principle that guided Donald Miller's life was that the world would improve if individuals accepted their own agency to live a better story and that all challenges could produce a blessing. He felt this as a calling from God and chose to serve God by joining Him in the process of creation.

Don's company, Business Made Simple, helped business leaders discover what was wrong with their businesses and gave them the simple frameworks they needed to keep those businesses growing. His company certified more than five thousand business coaches and marketing consultants to help business leaders grow their companies.

Before he died, Don wrote more than twenty books. He wrote memoirs, business books, novels, and even a book of poetry about life with his family at Goose Hill.

Don provided his children with love, security, and an example to follow. As a husband, Don supported his wife by being a constant encourager and never losing track of what a gift he'd been given in his family.

Don never let the ambitious stories he wanted to live come before the love story he got to experience with Betsy.

JOAN FREEMAN

Joan Freeman was known for teaching her neighbors how to grow a vegetable garden. Each house on her street was given a small, raised bed in the field beside her house, and each season she'd visit families and help them plot their summer garden. Looking back, though, we realized she had little interest in gardening at all. Joan loved people and loved to see how much they grew season after season. She knew that people, like plants, flourished when tended to. Each summer, she'd establish workdays where all the families would come together to share the workload of tending the garden.

Many of the families on her street now credit those days to the deep friendships that they have established in the neighborhood, and some parents even credit Joan for creating much-needed time with their own busy children. Each year, her neighborhood enjoyed a peak season feast where they'd eat from the produce they grew. Joan is survived by her husband of thirty-seven years and their two adult children, who have created community gardens in their own neighborhoods. Above all, Joan valued time with family and friends, nourishing conversations, the joy of fresh food, and the bounty of hard work. After her funeral services on Thursday, the neighborhood will dedicate the community garden in her name with a sign and plaque. The Joan Freeman Community Garden will now be tended by a board of directors made up of family members from Joan's neighborhood.

MATTHEW CORNELIUS

Matthew Cornelius leaves behind a legacy of family, terrific friendships, and fly fishing.

In his midforties, Matthew and his wife decided to quit their jobs, sell their home and possessions, and buy an abandoned retreat center in Montana. It was there that Matthew began leading fly-fishing trips down local rivers, pouring himself into groups of executives from businesses and nonprofits he believed were changing the world.

Hundreds expressed their condolences and recalled long conversations in fishing boats during which Matthew, over and over, proved himself a terrific listener and encourager.

Matthew leaves behind his wife and two children, all of whom are avid fishers and each, in their own right, terrific listeners and encouragers.

SARA CARTER

Sara Carter raised over $1 million for charity by running more than twenty-five marathons.

A running coach at Harris High School, she inspired countless students to do hard things for great reasons.

Sara ran a local publicity campaign for each race, stopping by the small-town paper, hosting dinners, showing up to speak at churches, and even giving her presentation at the local senior center. In her presentation, she would highlight a local charity and introduce her network to the work these organizations were doing. Then, she'd raise money and run the race, always taking a runner with her who either worked at the charity or was being benefited by it.

Her tireless work promoting good in the world changed an entire community. Nonprofits began to network with one another and share best practices. City leaders began working with charities to enhance their reach and capabilities. And the local police precinct credited a drop in crime to Sara's efforts to combat poverty.

Sara leaves behind a husband and three children who were each surrogates for her causes and all of whom ran multiple marathons with their wife and mother. Her family requests that, in lieu of flowers, make a donation to Sara's foundation, which matches the donations of other runners for charitable causes.

These eulogies are much more than creative, reflective assignments. They are narrative strategies. They are plans. What I mean by that is your mind will begin to move in the direction your eulogy has defined, almost naturally. The more you read your eulogy, the more cognitive dissonance will be created in your mind and the more you will want to resolve that dissonance by actually making those stories happen.

Of course, you can edit your eulogy any time you want to make it more realistic, more interesting and inspiring, or even to change it completely. If you read your eulogy and it makes you interested in your own story, you're doing it right.

Don't be surprised if much of what you've written in your eulogy comes true. When I was just fifteen, a guest speaker came to our high school and asked us to write a letter to a friend describing what our lives would be like twenty years in the future. He gave us twenty minutes and I fired off a letter about all I wanted to accomplish. I grew up in Texas where the summers were hot, so I decided I wanted to live in Oregon, a state I thought bordered Canada (I flunked geography if you can believe it), and that I'd write *New York Times* bestselling books and I'd own my own business.

I gave that letter to a friend and, no kidding, twenty years later she found the letter in a box in her attic. Knowing I'd become a bestselling author, she called to confirm I actually lived in Oregon and had started a business. And you guessed it, it had all come true.

At the time, I only had a vague memory of writing that letter, but since then I've come to believe in the power of writing down your vision. I don't believe writing down a vision for your life creates any sort of magic in the universe, but I do believe it sets a general compass for your subconscious. Then, when you move out into the world, you make decisions that align with the set vision. As a result, you make progress toward your goal.

Recently, one of our business coaches, Tony Everett, took the eulogy exercise into a juvenile detention center in California. Tony runs an organization called Pure Games, which uses sports to teach character building in schools and detention centers. Tony told me that in the detention centers, kids often come from difficult backgrounds and family dynamics. Most of the kids in juvenile detention, he said, have been abandoned.

As the kids wrote their eulogies, I was struck that every single one of them talked about how they wanted to be a good parent, how they would be faithful to their spouse, and how they would be there for their children. It was as though they wanted to live lives that would stop the cycle they'd been spun into:

Mark was always loving and caring and funny. Mark was a great husband who would do anything to make his wife happy. He was an even better father who would give the world to his son. Also a great son and grandson who made his family proud by making it out of the streets and leaving an amazing legacy. He became one of the greatest entrepreneurs known to man and established a business for his family to continue even when he was gone. Mark always knew how to make someone smile and help others out.

And . . .

Angel was always a good and loving father and a hardworking and respectful man. He always made sure his family had food and that they felt safe. He also made his own company and now everyone knows his clothing brand. Angel always loved to spend time with his family playing games, laughing, and going out to places like the time he took everyone to Hawaii.

I got choked up reading through the eulogies because the same thing will likely happen to these kids that will happen to you and me. When it comes time to make a good or bad decision, we will remember our story, the story we defined for ourselves, and we will ask ourselves whether the scene we're about to live out belongs in the story or not.

And that's really the key, isn't it? When we imagine our life as a movie and begin making decisions that will make the movie more meaningful and more interesting, we will build a more compelling life. When we ask ourselves, "If a character in a movie did this, would I respect that character?" we find a deeper place of wisdom and set ourselves up for a greater life experience.

Fate doesn't have to write our story, at least not all of it. We get to direct our own stories. We get to establish the vision and put a little something on the plot every day. We do not have to be victims stuck in a story written dispassionately by chance. If we make a plan and we review that plan in a morning ritual, we are much more likely to live a fulfilling life and experience a deep sense of meaning.

Take some time and complete the first exercise in the Hero on a Mission Life Plan and morning ritual. Write your eulogy.

In the back pages of this book, as well as online at HeroOnAMission .com, you can create your eulogy and then review it each day as part of your morning ritual. Your eulogy is the primary tool to help you create narrative traction.

11

· · · · · · · · · · · · · ·

Cast Your Long-Term and Short-Term Visions

I HOPE THE EULOGY ASSIGNMENT was life giving. Often, just the establishment of a vision can give you a sense of hope, especially combined with a belief in your own agency to accomplish that vision.

Often, though, writing your eulogy and establishing a vision for your life leaves you wondering where to start. You may even feel your eulogy was too ambitious and accomplishing such a terrific life seems unattainable.

You will not feel that way after you finish the second assignment in the Hero on a Mission Life Plan: casting a ten-year, five-year, and one-year vision.

A HERO ON A MISSION TAKES IT ONE STEP AT A TIME

Once a storyteller knows where they want their story to go, they plan the moments that will drive their character closer and closer to the climactic scene.

While driving the story forward, though, a storyteller has to be careful not to "lose the plot." What I mean when I say "lose the plot" is that the story has to be about something and the best way to make it about something is to not make it about anything else.

Good writing is not an exercise in addition; it's an exercise in subtraction. Great storytellers tell great stories because they know what to leave out.

We've all watched a movie or two that has lost the plot. At the beginning we see a hero who wants something, but after a half hour or so the movie picks up on another character and then another and the story fails to come back to the first character. Then we find the secondary characters unreliable and perhaps even unlikeable, and our brains get tired of having to pay attention to so many different plotlines. So we check out.

Typically, the story stopped being interesting because the writer started off on a certain path, but then had a "great idea" that took the story in a different direction. Later, they just couldn't edit some of those "great scenes" out even though they didn't serve the original plot.

In writing, there's an appropriate saying: "Kill your darlings." It's a reminder that no matter how much you like a character, a scene, or a story line, if it doesn't serve the plot, it has to go.

Again, life can sometimes feel similar to the experience of sitting in a theater watching a movie that is anything but cohesive. Several times each year, I find myself in situations that don't serve the plot I've determined for my life. Either I've flown to another city to sit in on a meeting that somebody else thought I "just couldn't miss" only to realize that while the people I'm with are working on something interesting, it has nothing to do with the change I'm trying to bring into the world, or, worse, I find myself diving into a project because I wanted to please somebody at the cost of losing traction in my own story.

Regardless, knowing what our story is going to be about and writing a eulogy to memorialize that story are not quite enough to ensure we maintain focus.

What we need are some baby steps. We need to write down some scenes that will pull us into the story and ensure it is attempting to support the theme we've determined for our lives.

Of course, we can't control everything, nor should we. Life often throws us opportunities to experience something magical. If we are too controlling about our lives' stories, we might miss those experiences. Sometimes fate lends us a tailwind. But we can only be grateful for a tailwind if it is helping us get to where we want to go.

To help you get where you want to go, we've included three worksheets that will allow you to turn your long-term vision into short, easy-to-execute phases.

While our eulogy is a great centering tool, it often feels like we are projecting so far into the future that we may as well be describing somebody else. But when we create a vision that is limited to ten years, five years, and one year, we have a direction in which we can live our lives that aligns with the long-term vision we created in our eulogy assignment.

YOU'RE GOING TO TRANSFORM, SO YOU MIGHT AS WELL TRANSFORM IN THE RIGHT DIRECTION

Before Betsy and I moved to Goose Hill, we lived in a small house in which I didn't have a good office. I decided to have a shed built in the backyard that I could use as a writing retreat. It was a tiny, ten-by-twelve room with no bathroom or running water. It had a desk, a chair, and a bookshelf. And it quickly became my favorite place.

I wrote a couple books in that shed. Around the outside, I had trellises attached to the siding, and around the windows the trellises made a frame. The entire shed looked like a cage of high-end chicken wire.

Around the bottom of the shed I planted Carolina jessamine, a strong, fast-growing vine that flowers yellow in the spring and fall. Over the years, I clipped the vines and trained them to grow up the trellises. After only a few years, the shed looked like a big green box made of leaves and flowers. Vines even made their way inside. The jessamine pierced through the wood and sheetrock and wound around inside the window and down the curtains behind my desk. The shed was beautiful to look at and I liked it because it reminded me that healthy things grow.

You and I are like Carolina jessamine. As the years go by, we transform and hopefully grow into a better version of ourselves. Just like the jessamine around my shed, though, if we don't train our growth, we will develop in disparate directions. If we don't decide the direction in which our stories will be lived, we may live in confusion and choke out other plants in the garden, rip into the walls of our lives, or lie thick around the ground. All because we never found something to cling to and climb.

The ten-year, five-year, and one-year vision exercises are like those trellises: the more care you take to determine the direction of your growth, the more likely your life will look the way you want by the time your story is over.

THE TEN-YEAR, FIVE-YEAR, AND ONE-YEAR VISION WORKSHEETS

The second assignment in the HOAM Life Plan is to fill out the ten-year, five-year, and one-year worksheets.

Each vision worksheet is the same. Start with the ten-year vision and work your way backward to the one-year vision.

As you fill in the worksheets, you are likely to discover that what you think you can get done in ten years is considerable, but when you fill out the five-year and one-year worksheets, you may realize you have been too aspirational.

By the time you get to the one-year vision worksheet, you realize living a great story is going to require immediate action. It's this sense that you need to take immediate action in your life that will create the narrative traction we're looking for. The truth is, to live a good story we are going to have to make progress almost every day. Otherwise fate will take control. And remember, fate isn't conspiring for you and it isn't conspiring against you. It simply is. You, on the other hand, have a will and can affect what your future looks like.

While the eulogy is an exercise in dreaming and hoping, these worksheets are more practical. In order to make a dream come true, we've got to pick up a hammer and do some work. These sheets will help you know what work you need to do.

The vision sheets look like this:

My Life Plan Ten-Year Vision

If a movie was made about your life this year, what would it be called?	Age
_____	_____

Career	Health
• _____	• _____
• _____	• _____
• _____	• _____

Family	Friends
• _____	• _____
• _____	• _____
• _____	• _____

Spiritual	
• _____	• _____
• _____	• _____

2 things I try to do every day	2 things I don't do
• _____	• _____
• _____	• _____

The central theme of my story at this point is

_____

After you finish this chapter, you can create your ten-year, five-year, and one-year visions. Or you can finish the book and then create your entire life plan in one focused process. You can use the back pages of this book, print out a larger version of the life plan and daily planner, or join the community and use the online software at HeroOnAMission.com.

Again, the ten-year, five-year, and one-year worksheets are the same. You will simply complete the same assignment three times.

Once you're finished, you will have four pages of material to review in your morning ritual. First, you'll read your eulogy, then you'll review your ten-year, five-year, and one-year worksheets.

Reviewing these pages, along with your daily planner page, will increase the amount of narrative traction you experience in your life. You will wake up morning after morning more and more interested in your own story.

To help you perform this exercise, I'll break down each section. Again, the three worksheets are all the same, so once you fill out the ten-year, move on and do the same exercise for the five-year and one-year sheets.

Here are the various parts of the vision worksheets explained:

WHAT'S THE TITLE OF YOUR MOVIE?

If a movie was made about your life this year, what would it be called?

_____

Each vision worksheet gets a movie title. There are a couple of good reasons I ask you to create a movie title for the next three seasons of your life. The first is to remind you that your life is a narrative that moves forward in time and is supposed to be about something. The second is because, not unlike your eulogy, the "title" of your story will help your vision come to life in your imagination.

When you choose the title for each of your vision sheets, imagine your life ten years from now, five years from now, and one year from now. Then come up with a fictional movie title that describes that person and who they have become.

Remember, you're looking into the future. You might not be the person you want to be now, but we've got to pick a point on the horizon to head toward; otherwise we won't know what direction in which to transform.

My ten-year vision movie title is _Fearless Leader_. I chose this because as a kid my mother hung one of those plaques on my bedroom wall that explains the meaning of your name. Under "Donald Miller" were printed the words "Fearless Leader." I can still remember looking at that plaque, convinced they'd gotten it wrong. I was anything but a leader and anything but fearless. But over the years, I kept taking leadership opportunities because I felt like I was supposed to become a fearless leader.

Sometimes I think they just put whatever they want on those plaques to trick kids into making something of their lives. If that's the case, I'm grateful. Believing I was supposed to become a fearless leader shaped my entire life because it caused me to look for and step into more and more leadership responsibilities.

Still, I have some transforming to do. To accomplish my goals in life, I'm going to have to develop even more courage. Raising a family, growing a company, and even writing more books means I have to continue to believe in my own voice and that my ideas matter.

In a way, every hero on a mission must transform into a fearless leader.

My five-year movie title is *Building a Legacy* because I'm realizing more that I can't take my story with me; I have to leave it behind with Emmeline and Betsy. I want them to have a strong sense of positive identity in the family they helped create, and I want to do my part.

My one-year movie title is *Focused on a Firm Foundation* because there are more distractions in my life than ever and yet what I do in the coming year will be the foundation for the next twenty. There is a lot of content for my company that needs to be created. For the next twelve months, I need to work hard. More specifically, I need to work hard on the right things.

On my way to becoming a fearless leader, I'll have to pass through a couple other stories and benchmarks in my personal transformation. I'll have to stay focused and get to work, and I'll have to build a legacy with the people I love. The vision worksheets and story titles will guide me just as the trellises on my old writing shed guided the vines.

I have decided what direction I want to grow. Inasmuch as I can control my life and accept my own agency, I'll grow into the trellises I've built in my three worksheets.

WRITE DOWN YOUR AGE AND CREATE SHORT-TERM DEADLINES

The next box on your worksheet gives you space to write down how old you will be ten years, five years, and one year from now.

It's strange to look at my ten-year vision sheet and read the number "59." When we are kids, we think kids are born kids and old people are born old. You hardly process the fact that you are going to become older yourself. The truth is that the pages in our stories are flipping toward the end whether or not we write anything good on them. Realizing that the clock is ticking on your story is a tough but beautiful part of growing up. Acknowledging that our stories will someday end makes the need to take action more urgent.

When we write down how old we will be in ten years, five years, and one year, we more fully accept the truth: the blank pages of our story are turning, and we have the agency to write something interesting on them. This becomes especially true the day you wake up and the number on your ten-year worksheet is only nine years away! The clock is indeed ticking.

As you review your life plan in your daily ritual, reading how old you will be in ten years, five years, and one year enhances the psychological effect of a ticking clock that will create more narrative traction in your story.

MINE THE SUBPLOTS AND YOU'LL TELL A GREAT STORY

Another area in which the vision worksheets will help is to identify the subplots in your overall story and mine them for the best possible result.

Subplots keep the story moving along at a pace quick enough so that the audience doesn't lose interest.

When you go to a movie, you may think you are watching a story. But you aren't. What you're actually watching is a series of short stories that are stitched together by an overarching plot.

For instance, if the plot in the story is about a guy who wants to run a marathon, there may be a subplot about his career and how he's intimidated by his physically fit boss who chides him for the spare tire around his waist. There might be a subplot about his girlfriend who has been waiting years for a ring and is beginning to think he's a deadbeat. There could also be a subplot about how he bonded with his father over hot dogs, nachos, and baseball games for years, but now he has to make a change that could disrupt that bond.

Subplots are great as long as they contribute to the overall plot.

Your eulogy defined the overall plot of your life story, but your subplots will act like short stories within that plot. Your subplots will give your story the diversity it needs to remain interesting.

The worksheets define a few subplots most of us have in common.

Career
· _____
· _____
· _____

Health
· _____
· _____
· _____

Family
· _____
· _____
· _____

Friends
· _____
· _____

Spiritual
· _____   · _____
· _____   · _____

Establishing subplots in your story will help you compartmentalize your ambitions so that you will know the different projects happening in various areas of your life.

In my career subplot, for instance, I set financial goals for my company. I also included the various books I'm writing and even "side projects" I'm working on with friends.

In the category of physical goals, I'd like to be able to bike one hundred miles again in a single day. For family goals, I wrote down that I wanted to be present and do a good bit of the work it takes to raise an infant. I also included that I would become a terrific cook, which is a hobby I've recently become excited about.

My community goals involve deepening the advisory board community I've started and continuing to host events at Goose Hill.

My spiritual goals revolve around my morning routine. During that ritual, I take time to pray for Betsy, Emmeline, and my close friends.

Each of these subplots is really its own story. But because they all fit in the overall narrative for my life (which is to help people create and live better stories) my life feels like it makes sense. There are certainly times I get too busy. But being too busy is easy enough to manage. It's being too busy in the wrong direction that feels miserable.

Keeping my subplots aligned with my overall life mission saves me from living a story that has lost its plot.

A HERO TRANSFORMS BY TAKING ACTION

So far, our vision sheets have been about dreaming and planning. But in a story, the hero has to take action. There aren't many movies about two people sitting at a table talking about life. An audience needs to see physical movement in order to stay interested in the story.

In literature, too, you'll find great writers using active language, bounding with action verbs. Characters *throw* off their bedsheets and *slide* into their slippers, *yelping* at the cold water in the shower before they *pull* on their trousers, *cinch* their belt, and *slurp* their coffee, *fumbling* themselves out the door while *throwing* their free hand up to hail a cab.

In stories and in life, characters must take action. I know this is a book and you are likely sitting down to read it, but hopefully when you're finished, you will start moving into your mission with force.

We will not transform by thinking and dreaming. We will transform by doing.

At the bottom of your vision worksheet, I've included a place where you can write down two actions that you will commit to doing every day. For me, I'm committed to exercising for at least twenty minutes and writing something every day.

Of course you will also take action on your task lists and appointments. You'll be writing those down in the daily planner I'll introduce you to soon. But having two actions you will take every day ensures consistent movement in a positive direction.

The actions you're looking to take should be simple to execute, repeatable, and most important, foundational. By foundational I mean the actions you will take will be the lead in a string of dominoes. If I get up early and write every day, it means I get my foundational work done. Even if I just write a few paragraphs, the consistent, daily action means that by the time my funeral rolls around, I will have written more than twenty books, which is the vision I wrote down in my eulogy.

Not only that, but the actions I am taking to move myself forward have a domino effect in other areas of my life. For example, by getting up early to write, I am more likely to skip that glass of whiskey the night before and get a better night's sleep. In fact, after I defined the daily action of getting up to write, I've nearly stopped drinking altogether. This has benefited my sleep, my health, and my writing. In other words, if I get up early and write every day, my entire life settles into a healthy rhythm.

Getting exercise is similarly effective. Just twenty minutes of heart-pounding exercise each day (I walk the hills around Goose Hill and I swim) makes me healthier, but also gives me twenty more minutes to reflect (I come up with my best ideas while on walks) and I'm more likely to eat better because feeling sluggish while on a walk is no fun. It also ensures that I've taken care of my heart that day and will live a little longer with Betsy and the baby.

I confess I am much more consistent with the writing than I am with the exercise. I write about five days each week and exercise between two to three times each week. Regardless, I give myself an enormous amount of grace. Even though I want to do these things every day, the fact I do them several times each week puts me way ahead of the pace I would have maintained had I not determined my two daily actions.

If you skip a few days and start feeling guilty, your life plan will become a tool that shames you and it will be worthless because you will likely quit. Instead, have some grace, allow the daily tasks to determine a direction, and try to head in that direction as many days as possible. A life plan should not judge you; it should guide you and even encourage you.

What are two actions you would like to take every day that will organize and structure your life for a better chance at achieving the vision you've established in your eulogy?

Take time to decide two things you will try to do every day and include them in your vision worksheets.

If you want those actions to evolve over time, they can get more and more ambitious in the five- and ten-year worksheets.

For instance, this year you may want to take a daily walk, but five years from now you may want to run three miles each day. As you review your worksheets, you will know that the walks you are taking need to evolve into jogs.

2 things I try to do every day	2 things I don't do	
• _____ • _____	• _____ • _____	

A HERO TRANSFORMS BY DECIDING WHAT *NOT* TO DO TOO

Equally as important as taking action is restraint. The vision worksheets ask you what unhealthy activities or actions you will no longer perform.

The two things I decided to stop doing were eating sweets and talking about people in a demeaning way.

If I don't eat sugar, I feel better, write more words, am more present in important conversations, and am healthier. If I don't talk about people in a demeaning way, even if they may seemingly deserve it, I am more positive and don't feel like a hypocrite for talking about somebody behind their back.

This is one of the ways I limit how much time the villain inside me spends on the stage. Villains stew over their enemies and demean others as a way of feeling powerful themselves. I want to avoid that behavior as much as possible.

Are there things in life that you simply refuse to do? Do your values show up in your actions?

The actions I don't take have proven to be just as or more effective as the actions I take. Even though I have a strong bias toward action, I'd actually say it's the restraint that has changed my life the most. I want to speak about people in a positive way. Certainly there are bad people out there whose evil deeds deserve to be disclosed in an effort to warn others. But for the most part, life goes better when we choose to see the best in others.

Regardless of the two things you choose to do every day and the two areas where you choose to show restraint, the idea here is to begin taking action to become a better version of yourself.

When a hero lives into the challenge set before them, they begin to transform. In order to accomplish the things you've written down in your vision sheets, you will have to become an entirely different person.

As I said earlier, victims and villains do not transform. A victim may be rescued but they do not transform. And a villain is the same dastardly person at the end of the story as they were at the beginning. It's the hero on a mission who transforms.

A HERO HAS NO TIME FOR NIHILISM

The greatest benefit of creating your HOAM plan is that it will save you from a life that feels meaningless.

The more you review that plan, the more you will avoid the existential vacuum Viktor Frankl warns us about.

You will never see an action hero look into the camera and say, "I'm bored."

The characters Denzel Washington, Matt Damon, Gal Gadot, and Liam Neeson play are too busy trying to save the world to be bored.

Nihilists believe life is meaningless and there is no reason to get up and make change. Find me a nihilist, though, and I'll show you a person who has become bored with life. They do not have a vision. They do not have an internal locus of control. They do not accept their own agency.

The truth? Nihilists have too much time on their hands.

I don't mean that as an insult. If you try to figure out the meaning of life and the purpose of humanity from a strictly philosophical perspective, you're likely to become a nihilist. Friedrich Nietzsche, Jean-Paul Sartre, Simone de Beauvoir, and Søren Kierkegaard are all considered nihilists. Those folks are a lot smarter than me, so God bless them. I don't believe life was only meant to be studied and figured out, though. I believe it was mostly meant to be lived. There's nothing romantic about holding the hand of your lover while softly explaining the brain science of what is happening between you. It's way more fun to just make out.

Again, meaning is only experienced in motion. Your vision worksheets will help you home in on exactly what direction to live and what actions to take.

Nihilism and a haunting sense of fatalism are luxuries people experience when they are mostly sedentary. A surgeon does not ponder the futility of life while they are transplanting a heart. They are too busy saving a life to ponder the meaning of life. They are too busy experiencing meaning to debate its merit.

The point is this: Act. Build something meaningful. Plan your mission and fight distractions so you can put something on the plot of your life story.

Your eulogy and vision worksheets will help you better understand what you want your story to be about. And the next two tools will put something on the plot and make it happen.

In the next couple of chapters, we will talk about how to set goals as part of your action plan. Then, finally, I'll show you a daily planner page that will bring it all together.

12

. . . .

A Hero Gets Things Done

ON YOUR VISION WORKSHEET, you likely listed some projects you wanted to bring into the world. You wanted to write a book or start a business or grow a garden.

The third (and optional) step in creating your life plan and experiencing a life of meaning is to fill out your goal-setting worksheets.

The reason I say these goal-setting worksheets are optional is because they might not be necessary for you.

Your ten-year, five-year, and one-year visions may be enough to help you create narrative traction and live each day with focus and intention.

Nevertheless, there have been many occasions, especially when I'm starting something new, when it benefits me to set a goal. I also use the goal-setting worksheets to get my mind around major projects.

That said, I don't review my goals every day in my morning ritual. At best I review them once each week. The reason for this is because my vision worksheets are enough to keep me motivated. By reviewing my goal-setting worksheets only once each week, my morning ritual is a little shorter. And because it's shorter, I perform it more often.

Nevertheless, as we've already established, living a story is about taking action. But what are we going to take action on?

Right now, I have several goals. The fact that you are reading this book means I achieved at least one of them. I've three more books to write once I'm done with this one. Each of those is a goal.

Goose Hill was once spelled out on a goal-setting worksheet. Now it exists, or at least it mostly exists. I've used the worksheet to imagine new business divisions and even new communities.

Completing projects and achieving goals, though, is going to require some strategy.

REACHING A GOAL REQUIRES A PLAN

One reason we don't reach our goals is because we think setting a goal and writing it down will magically cause us to achieve it. But goals don't get achieved just because we write them down. We need to implement a strategy.

Years ago, when I moved from Portland to D.C. to date Betsy, I sold everything I owned and bought a Volkswagen camping van. For a few years in the '90s, Volkswagen rereleased their camping van, decked out with a tent-top bed, sink, and rear bench. I figured this would likely be Lucy's and my last big adventure before we settled down to married life.

For the trip, I purchased every audio book I could find on goal setting, willpower, and self-discipline. I didn't go the self-help direction, though. I downloaded books by psychologists and neuroscientists. I wasn't looking for inspiration as much as I was looking for ways to hack my own brain and get more done.

I can't remember how many books I listened to on the subject, but it's a big country and I absorbed the material from coast to coast. Lucy and I cruised through the Southwest jamming out to essays on brain chemistry.

Lucy didn't get a lot out of it, but that's because she's generally satisfied with life as it is. I, on the other hand, learned a great deal.

Yet, there was a problem: the books I listened to weren't practical. Sometimes psychologists and researchers have a tough time applying their findings to actionable tasks. What I needed was a worksheet I could fill out that would help me apply the research.

The goal-setting worksheet along with the planner pages I'll introduce you to in the next chapter are the result of the personal strategy I came up with on that road trip.

Goal name	

Why does this goal matter to you?	Completion date

Goal partners

Milestones ❶ ❷ ❸

Daily sacrifices

Repetition record

SEVEN ELEMENTS THAT HELP YOU REACH YOUR GOALS

As you think about the projects you want to complete and the goals you want to set, consider the following elements.

Element #1: Know Why the Goal Matters

The first question on the worksheet is: "Why does this goal matter to you?" I ask that because when we understand the deeper reason for wanting to reach a goal, we connect it to our personal narrative.

For instance, if we set a goal to be debt free, it's just a numeric goal. But when we remind ourselves that when we become debt free we can take longer family vacations and afford to send our kids to college, we are more likely to make it happen.

> **Why does this goal matter to you?**
>
> _____

When we ask why a goal matters, we're really asking, "What are the stakes?" In stories, stakes are a significant tool that help an audience gain narrative traction.

The idea is to be definitively aware of what can be won or lost if we do or do not reach our goal.

If we remove the stakes from a story, we make it uninteresting. If Liam Neeson flies over the ocean to rescue another one of his daughters from kidnappers, only this time he discovers it was a college prank played on his daughter and so the final ninety minutes of the movie show Liam and his daughter sitting in a café talking about whether or not she should go to grad school, the movie is essentially a dud.

Using your morning ritual to remind yourself why your goal matters will increase the chances you will follow through.

Element #2: Completion Date

Deadlines help us reach our goals. As we discussed when we wrote our eulogies and calculated how much longer we have to live, a deadline ramps up urgency.

Again, what we are looking for both in our lives and in our goals is narrative traction. Knowing our why and knowing when we need to have the goal accomplished causes our brain to further engage in the story.

On your goal-setting worksheet, write down when you expect to accomplish your goal.

Writing down our hopeful completion date will start the countdown clock. Every morning when we review our goal, we will hear the clock ticking louder and louder. Because of this, you'll be more interested and more driven to accomplish your goals.

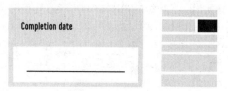

Element #3: Goal Partners

Knowing our why and creating a deadline are terrific tools to help us reach a goal. But we can increase our narrative traction even further by setting and reaching our goals in the context of community.

A goal partner is an individual or a group of people who walk alongside you, attempting to accomplish the exact same goal.

I'm not talking about accountability partners. I'm talking about people who will set the exact same goal and enter into the story with you so you aren't traveling alone.

Think about it. If we want to lose twenty pounds, we can establish our why along with a deadline. And about a week later we'll be ordering extra pepperoni on our pizza.

But let's say you call a few friends who have mentioned that they want to get into shape. You invite them to dinner and explain that you want to accomplish the goal as a group. You give yourselves six months to get it done, then you each put a hundred dollars into a jar with the understanding that anybody who loses the twenty pounds gets their hundred dollars back, plus any extra money left over from the people who don't accomplish the goal. Then you agree to meet at the park at 7:00 a.m. on Saturdays for the next six months to walk three miles and share best practices along with encouragement.

That plan is obviously more likely to work. After all, we are social beings. We travel further together than we do alone. We care about what other people think about us. We will work harder for our friends and family than we will work for personal benefit alone.

The key here is to create a community around the goal. Do you want to double the size of your business? Do you want to find a better job? Whatever your goal, start a community that is focused on achieving that goal together. Find partners who will accomplish your goal with you, and you dramatically increase your chances of hitting that goal.

Element #4: Milestones

It's often hard to stay motivated when you can't see the top of the mountain. Losing twenty pounds or starting a business can feel like a monumental challenge.

What will help on a large goal, then, are milestones. When we break our goal up into smaller pieces, we can see our progress coming toward us and we have reasons to celebrate along the way.

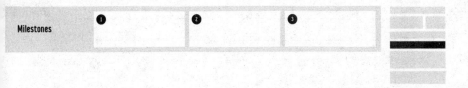

Every year at my company, we establish a one-year financial goal followed by twelve monthly goals. We even set revenue goals per revenue stream, breaking those down into twelve milestones as well.

Breaking a large goal down into milestones not only helps us celebrate the pass-through wins, but it also makes the goal more accessible. Filling out the paperwork to start a business, then creating the website, then making and shipping our first product sounds less intimidating than "starting a business."

As you review your milestones, you will be able to see where you're going and where you've been. You'll also get good optics on your progress. This will increase your morale as you encounter challenges. There's nothing like a little progress to increase our sense of hope.

Element #5: Daily Sacrifices

Many people think writing down their goal is some kind of magical process that will ensure success.

Of course this isn't true. The only reason we have to set goals in the first place is because they require sacrifices that we would rather not make. There is no magical solution to get around it; otherwise reaching goals would be easy.

What we need is a specific understanding of the daily sacrifice that will be required to achieve our goal.

If I want to get out of credit card debt, for instance, my daily sacrifice may be to put ten dollars into savings. Then, once a

Daily sacrifices

_____

_____

month, I would use that three hundred or so dollars to pay down my debt. After a year or so, perhaps my debt will be gone.

If my goal is to grow my new business, my daily sacrifice might be to pick up the phone and make two cold calls every day.

Heroes accept that things worth achieving require sacrifice. Victims, on the other hand, do not believe they have the ability to sacrifice because they are trapped and without power or agency.

The key is to make a daily sacrifice that, over time, will add up to significant progress.

In the "Daily Sacrifice" section of the goal-setting worksheet, write down your daily sacrifice so you have more clarity on the small, daily cost of your goal.

Element #6: Repetition Record

After we decide what our daily sacrifice will be, we can turn our goal-setting exercise into a game by keeping score.

At the bottom of our goal-setting worksheet, we have a "Repetition Record" that will allow us to check a box for every day we perform our daily sacrifice.

If we check off a couple boxes on consecutive days, we're likely to find that we want to improve that streak by going one

Repetition record

more day and then another day after that. If we fail one day, of course, we can just start another streak.

This is another lesson I learned from Jerry Seinfeld. He started putting an X on his calendar every day that he accomplished a specific task. He found that, over time, he was performing the task more to add an X than to actually achieve the task. He didn't want to break his streak. Nevertheless, the accomplishment of the task bettered his life. He'd turned a good habit into a game with a scoreboard.

Element #7: Set No More Than Three Goals at a Time

The final element is to have only three goals running at one time. If I want to ride my bike one hundred miles, pay off debt, and write a book, I'll set aside three goal-setting worksheets as a way of identifying my primary goals, separating them from the rest. I only move another goal up to the primary category when I accomplish one of the other primary goals.

I have about ten goal-setting worksheets filled out right now, but I only review three of them daily as part of my morning ritual.

The reason for this is because the brain has trouble concentrating on more than three priorities at a time. As soon as you add a fourth goal, you may as well have added twenty more because the brain will begin storing your priorities as random information in a metaphorical junk drawer.

HEROES TAKE ACTION

In movies, the camera follows the hero because the hero takes action and action is interesting. A hero moves. A hero does things. The goal-setting worksheet is designed to help you take action. Taking action on your goals will help you create a more meaningful life experience.

Achieving a challenging goal takes thoughtful planning and consistent commitment. I'm hopeful the goal-setting worksheet will help you establish your goals and follow through.

Next, let's look at a final tool that will help you create narrative traction: the daily planner.

13

. . . .

The Hero on a Mission
Daily Planner

FOR NEARLY FIFTEEN YEARS now, my life has been greatly improved by a simple, fifteen-minute task. I fill out my HOAM Daily Planner.

Before filling out my daily planner page, I am often slightly confused about what I should be working on that day. I may know I've got a meeting at 9:00 a.m., but it feels like there's something else I've got to be working on before 9:00 a.m. I know there were a few things I had to wrap up from yesterday, and also Betsy needs me to get something done around the house before we have company tonight. Because I'm not quite sure what my priorities are, I check my email to waste a little time and then I get off track because I'm sucked into some kind of problem-solving at work.

On a morning like this, my life looks a little like the junk drawer in the kitchen. It's as though everything I need to do has been thrown into the same compartment so that my priorities sit on top of one another without separation. The result is a lack of clarity.

The daily planner page guides you through a ten- to fifteen-minute exercise that creates extreme clarity about what's important and what's not, then it gives you a simple plan to get the most out of your day.

Not only this, but by filling out the planner you are reminded of the story you are likely to live, and therefore much less likely to let fate take the wheel. Filling out your daily planner page will activate your internal locus of control and ensure you're using your own agency to direct your life.

DIRECTING YOUR OWN STORY STEMS FROM A DAILY HABIT

Living a good story and reading a good story are two different things. Reading a good story is pleasurable because the writer has taken months, if not years, to get rid of all the stuff that shouldn't be in the story. Living a good story, then, is more like writing a good story. And writing a good story happens when a writer has created the disciplined habit of sitting down to do the work.

Last night when I met with my small business group, I was asked what it takes to write a book. Three of the members of the group want to write a book and each has an idea that could actually work.

My answer to the question "*What does it take to write a book?*" was this: Don't try to write a book; try to become somebody who enjoys writing every day.

If you try to write a book, you'll probably fail. But if you enjoy writing every day, you'll probably write several books.

There are millions of unwritten books out there. Their authors just didn't believe in themselves or their book enough to finish. It is true that 99 percent of writing is just the unwillingness to quit.

I don't want to call the unwillingness to quit *determination*, though. It may masquerade as determination, but the truth is that those who wake up and write good stories actually like the work. They like something that doesn't feel good. They like getting up early and ignoring their phone until a few more pages have been added. Life only feels good to them if they've put a little something on the plot.

That same enjoyment of writing a good story translates into living one. Good stories are not created in a day. It takes a routine, a daily discipline, and an enjoyment of that discipline so that it doesn't feel like discipline at all.

Inspiration will only take you so far. Show me a person who will do the work out of habit, even if they aren't particularly inspired, and I'll show you somebody who is destined for success.

A DAILY RITUAL

Once you have created your life plan, you get to review it every day in a morning ritual. This will help you maintain the narrative traction necessary to stay interested in your own story. And if you stay interested in your own story, you're more likely to experience a deep sense of meaning.

Beware, though, because it's easy to get distracted. Any ringing phone can and will take you off track. But it's the daily ritual that will bring you back into your own story, day after day. False starts are fine as long as you keep going.

The daily ritual, however, is not quite enough. We need some kind of planning mechanism to help us organize our thoughts and our progress.

THE HERO ON A MISSION DAILY PLANNER

The fourth assignment in the Hero on a Mission Life Plan is to fill out the Hero on a Mission Daily Planner. You can fill out the planner every day, or simply on days when you want to be more focused.

About fifteen years ago I created the daily planner to keep myself on track. I wanted it to include all the little tips and

Hero on a Mission Daily Planner

Date _____

☐ I've read my eulogy   ☐ I've reviewed my vision worksheets   ☐ I've reviewed my goals

Primary task one
_____
_____
_____
_____
_____

If you could live this day again, what would you do differently this time?
• _____
• _____
• _____

Primary task two
_____
_____
_____
_____
_____

What am I grateful for today?
• _____
• _____
• _____
• _____

Appointments
• _____
• _____
• _____
• _____
• _____

Secondary tasks
☐ _____   ☐ _____
☐ _____   ☐ _____
☐ _____   ☐ _____
☐ _____   ☐ _____

strategies I'd discovered to move the plot of my story forward. Over those fifteen years I wrote several books, started a family, built our dream house, launched a company, and more. I'd say the past fifteen years have been the exact opposite of the season I described at the beginning of this book. Before I created the planner, I was ambitious but without direction. The planner helps remind me what I'm supposed to be working on. As a result, I am able to accomplish more in less time.

Certainly there have been seasons when I've felt overworked, but those seasons are infrequent. Mostly I've just been able to filter out distractions and only work on what matters. In fact, none of us have to work all that hard to make our dreams come true. We just have to work on the right things and not work on the wrong things. And we have to do a little work every day. Again, heroes get up and put a little something on the plot every day while victims wait for fate to send a rescuer.

I've shared the planner with thousands of people and have been encouraged by the response. Creatives, especially, have found it useful. If you have trouble staying focused because there is so much vying for your attention, or if you have trouble remembering your priorities, you'll find the planner helpful.

I've included several free pages in the back of this book, or you can go to HeroOnAMission.com (or scan the QR code at the front of the book) to download larger pages you can hole-punch and turn into a planner. The daily planner includes eight simple sections to help you organize your day and take action in your story.

The point of the planner is to help you perform a morning ritual followed by a quick planning session in which you rein in the distractions to push your plot forward into another day. The daily page is going to help you tremendously.

You certainly don't have to fill out the planner every day, but the more days you perform the morning ritual, the fewer days you are likely to wander off into a mental fog.

Here are the eight elements of the planner you can fill out that will keep you on track:

Element #1: Review Your Eulogy

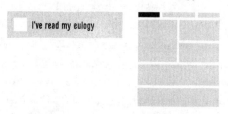

Your eulogy will help you gain narrative traction and act as a filter for the major decisions you make in life. Reviewing your eulogy will ensure you avoid the existential vacuum and remain interested and active in the development of your life story.

Element #2: Review Your Vision Worksheets

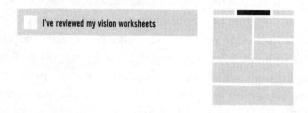

Reviewing your vision worksheets will remind you what you have decided your life will be about and will serve as a filter to help you make better decisions. Remember, the key to accomplishing something big is to stay focused on what you're trying to bring into the world and putting a little something on the plot every day.

If a writer forgets the plot of the story they are telling, then the story will wander into the weeds and the reader will feel lost. The less we review our life plans, the more likely we are to lose the plot of our own story.

Element #3: Review Your Goals

☐ I've reviewed my goals

When you review your goals, you're also reviewing the major projects you are working on, and you'll better understand what is a priority and what can wait.

If you've limited your goals to just three, you'll be able to do this quickly.

Element #4: Live from a Deep Place of Wisdom

If you could live this day again, what would you do differently this time?

- _____
- _____
- _____

If writing your eulogy was helpful in directing your life, imagine how powerful it would be to reflect on each day with a similar imaginative hindsight.

The next section of the planner will help you live from a deep place of wisdom by allowing you to preempt regret.

In the planner, I've included a simple question that causes us to reflect on what we can do to make fewer mistakes on a given day. The question is based on something Viktor Frankl used to tell his patients: "Live as if you were living a second time, and as though you had acted wrongly the first time."

It's a bit of a complex statement, but if you think about it, it's brilliant at summoning our own internal wisdom.

If, every morning, we pretended today were the second time we got to live this day and we could learn from the mistakes we made the first time, we'd have much more clarity on things such as the time we wasted, the relational neglect we committed, and the financial mistakes we made.

Each morning when I ask myself this question, I fast-forward to the end of that day and look back. I realize, from that perspective, I will have wanted to spend more time with Betsy, and I will have wanted to have set aside a couple hours to focus on the current writing project. I realize it would have been nice to stop and buy flowers, to send a thank-you card, to get some exercise.

Remember, victims are victims of their circumstances. Fate rules their lives. Outside forces dictate their every move. But when we surface our heroic energy, we gain control of our actions and use the power we have to live stories of meaning rather than regret.

If we don't have a morning exercise in which we stop, pull back from our limited perspective, and meditate on our own agency, we will move into autopilot and fate will once again blow our stories around in the wind.

Not only this, but if we make better decisions every day, the compound interest on those decisions will add up to a better life. Fast.

Each day, the daily planner will ask you to answer this question: *If you could live this day again, what would you do differently this time?*

Element #5: Determine Your Primary Tasks

Next, the planner will prompt you to prioritize your tasks.

One of the planner's most helpful functions is that it contains two different task lists: primary tasks and secondary tasks.

Your primary tasks are those large and important projects that will define your life. Those will be obvious after you review your ten-year, five-year, and one-year goals.

My primary tasks almost always involve creating content for a book or a business coaching session. My eulogy talks about having built a successful business coaching company. Therefore, during this phase of my life, I need to create helpful frameworks for business leaders.

So, for this season of my life, creating content needs to be my primary effort. In my primary tasks I'll write down the most important task I need to accomplish, followed by the second and the third.

Once I do this, I have immediate clarity on how to win the day. Regardless of what I fail to accomplish, if I get some work done on my primary tasks, I know the day will have moved my personal story forward. Not only will I have put something on the plot, but I'll have put something on the *right* plot.

Even though there is space for three primary tasks, I'd be lying if I said I accomplish all three each day. I rarely get to the third task. In fact, I often never get to the second. But it doesn't matter. The point is focus. If I work several hours on any of my primary tasks, I've made significant strides toward the life I've described in my eulogy.

Since I started identifying my primary tasks and getting a little work done on them each day, I've more than doubled my productivity. It used to take me nearly two years to write a book. Now I finish one every eight to ten months, and that's on top of the coaching materials I need to create.

Adding a baby to the mix has made it even more important for me to understand what the most important thing to work on is. Even though we've added an element of joyful chaos to the house, by knowing what I should be doing and what I can let go of, I can actually stay productive.

Knowing what your primary tasks are and making a little progress on them every day adds up. It may feel like slow going each day, but at the end of a month or a year, you'll be shocked at what you have accomplished.

Element #6: Use Gratitude to Fend Off Victim and Villain Mentalities

What I am grateful for today?

- _____
- _____
- _____
- _____

Taking time each morning to write down what we are grateful for creates a strong mental foundation for the rest of the day.

Victims are not grateful and for good reason. They are being mistreated, tortured, captured, and controlled.

Most of us, however, have plenty to be grateful for.

Like victims, villains aren't grateful either. You will never see a movie villain stop to reflect on how grateful they are for a friend, for a sip of water, or for such a lovely day as this. Gratitude connects us to others, acknowledges kindnesses, and places us in debt to the world. When we are grateful, we feel as though we owe the world a debt of gratitude and are inspired to return a kindness in the way we live our lives. Villains believe they are in debt to no one. Villains see the world as a competition for power. The world should be in debt to them; they will not be in debt to the world.

There is no single exercise more powerful to fend off victim and villain mentalities than one in which we acknowledge and even stimulate a feeling of gratitude.

Just last night I was tempted by victim mentality and used gratitude to recalibrate my perspective on life. After having a cup of ice cream, I willingly went into autopilot eating mode and had another. When I finished the second cup, I slumped into victim mentality. Why is sugar so hard to resist? I told myself I'd not eat sugar. Why am I such an idiot? I'm going to have a sugar hangover in the morning and yet I've got an important writing assignment. In other words: I'm a victim and life stinks.

I overcame that downward spiral by reminding myself that sometimes it feels good to indulge. Ice cream tastes fantastic.

And now I get to crawl into bed with my beautiful wife. I'll have the opportunity to swim off the calories tomorrow afternoon. I can still get up early and get some writing done. I am in a terrific position in life. Life is, in fact, fantastic. I love to swim and am grateful I have enough discipline to fend off the temptation of ice cream most of the time!

The victim mindset disappeared immediately.

Remember, victims and villains do not feel gratitude. So when we practice gratitude, we immediately transition out of victim and villain mentalities and become the hero capable of determining their own story and experiencing a deep sense of meaning.

The question you will want to answer in your daily planner, then, is: What are you grateful for today?

Besides fending off the lesser characters who exist within us, performing a gratitude reflection has even greater benefits. Gratitude, it turns out, helps us overcome procrastination.

Procrastinators subconsciously believe that a day full of miserable tasks they'd rather not do makes life "no fun," and nobody wants to endure a day that is no fun.

By reflecting on the things you are grateful for, such as exciting or restful things you get to do later in the day, you communicate to the subconscious that the day is not lost. When you reflect on what you're grateful for, you remember that later you will get to go for a walk or eat ice cream or enjoy dinner with friends. Right now, though, we've got to get to work.

Again, when we are grateful for all the things life has given us, we are more likely to sacrifice because we feel as though we owe life a little something in return.

When we are grateful, we remove a barrier keeping us from doing a little work that pushes our plot forward.

Element #7: Keep Track of Your Daily Appointments

The next exercise I perform is to transfer my daily appointments from my Google calendar to my daily planner.

Taking the time to write down (or retype into the online software) my appointments into my daily planner makes me more conscious of what I've decided to make happen for the rest of the day. In the printable version, by the way, we give you much more space for appointments.

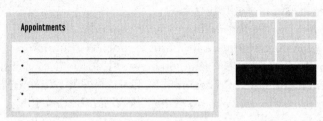

By transferring my appointments, I'm more conscious of whom I'm meeting, when I'm meeting with them, and why we're meeting. At the beginning of each day, rather than living in a tunnel in which I can see only what is next, I am aware of what all of my appointments are.

When you transfer your daily appointments to your planner, you will create a sense of clarity about what the day will look like, rather than feel as though you are starting your day out by walking into a fog.

Element #8: Manage Your Secondary Tasks

A hero has priorities. We've already established ours by listing our primary tasks. One of the hidden benefits of deciding what is important, though, is that in doing so we also define what is not important.

A hero does not stop to pick up their dry cleaning on the way to disarm the bomb.

Secondary tasks should never be confused with primary tasks. Picking up your dry cleaning isn't all that important. Sometimes heroes wear wrinkled clothes.

Unfortunately, your brain doesn't often know the difference between a primary and a secondary task.

For instance, Betsy and I moved into our house at Goose Hill about ten months ago. And though we've got the house mostly organized, the garage is a mess. I've only put away half the tools, we have no shelves or storage space, and there are boxes on the floor that are full, taped up, and unlabeled. I have no idea what is in those boxes.

Some people might walk through my garage and say, "You know, the state of a man's garage says a lot about them. An unorganized garage is a sign of an unorganized life."

I'd actually say the opposite is true in my case. Organizing my garage has been on my secondary task list for months. I've hardly lifted a finger. And I couldn't be happier about that.

Why? Because in those ten months I've written this book. And I shot a *How to Grow a Business* video course. And we had a baby and I've spent countless hours holding her and posting pictures on Instagram. All very important things. In fact, secondary tasks are not the things anybody will mention in our eulogy.

I can't imagine how sad a person's funeral would be if the highlight of their eulogy was the mention of a clean garage.

In all seriousness, though, writing down our secondary tasks reminds us of the things we need to get done later. Perhaps even tomorrow or the next day. When we don't write these tasks down, they bother us incessantly. We feel that we must do them now. But by writing them down and acknowledging them as secondary, we tell ourselves we haven't and won't forget them. It's just that we aren't going to do them right now.

As you plan your day, divide your tasks up into primary tasks and secondary tasks. You'll have greater clarity about what really needs to get done, and what you'll get done later.

Filling out your daily planner is meant to guide you through a morning ritual. As a culture, we've made a god out of productivity, but in doing so, too many of us have lost our own plot. We aren't experiencing meaning. The HOAM Daily Planner isn't about productivity, though it will certainly help you be more productive. Instead, it's designed to help you remember the plot of your story, stay interested and engaged in that story, and put a little something on the plot every day. The planner will help you gain narrative traction and experience a deep sense of meaning. Think of it as a morning ritual and enjoy filling it out with a cup of coffee. You will feel a great deal better about your life, your work, and your story.

14

. . . .

The Role That Matters Most

WHEN WE BOUGHT GOOSE Hill, it came with 970 trees. The land was thick with oak, ash, maple, cedar, and more than a few hackberry trees.

Sadly, the ash are dying. All the ash trees in Tennessee will be dead within ten years because of the emerald ash borer, a nonnative beetle that has spread across the region. Not only this, but our forest was overridden with a particular species of honeysuckle that spreads thick along the forest floor and drinks up all the water. This species of honeysuckle doesn't even give us a sweet-smelling flower, just dead trees in its wake.

It took three years to remove the honeysuckle. You have to cut the shrub at its base and poison it within thirty minutes of the cutting; and you have to do this every year for three years. This, however, preserved the forest. We've also identified the ash we want to save and have experts come each year to treat the trees we can afford to preserve. We've removed all the hackberry we can. The virtually useless tree grows fast and empty so that it gets tall and falls on other trees and houses and even people if they happen to be standing in the wrong place at the wrong time!

We've planted nearly a hundred native-species trees to more than replace those we lost in construction, and we have a team of arborists helping us protect the newly developed investment.

My favorite of the experts is a man named Peter Thevenot (pronounced TEV-a-no), a self-taught arborist who specializes in the art of espalier. More than thirty years ago, Peter retired from the business world to learn to train trees and shrubs to grow in patterns along a framework. He can grow a pear tree in a flat, straight line so that it looks like a fence or a vineyard-style row of grapes. Peter will grow a fence of pear trees around Betsy's garden.

When pruned and cared for correctly, an espaliered tree can live for more than one hundred years. Because they are pruned meticulously, more nutrients are available to create fruit. We will eat well at Goose Hill.

Peter is eighty now. He speaks in a coarse southern dialect that combines a Tennessee-tongued humility with a southern Louisiana spice. He wears a cowboy hat and has a mustache that makes him look a little like Richard Petty. Add to this that he smokes a pipe, dons long sleeves no matter the heat, talks slow, and seems to see through eyes that know. He looks at the land and knows where the trees will grow and where they will die.

Peter reminds me that wisdom does not grow fast. It only comes from experience and failure, from trial and error. Peter describes his job as painting with bark and leaves.

It takes four years for one of his trees to be ready for sale. It struck me as we walked the garden the other day that we weren't just adding trees around the garden, we were planting Peter's legacy.

When you meet somebody like Peter, you want to be like him—perhaps not in your knowledge of trees but certainly in your knowledge of something.

We have another friend who is helping us with Emmeline. Her name is Michelle Lloyd. When we first returned home from the hospital, we hired her as a newborn care specialist, allowing Betsy to recover from surgery. Michelle speaks with a delightful

New Zealand accent, but more important, she speaks baby. She has helped us understand that when Emmeline smacks her lip or chews her hand, she wants food. She taught us that when Emmeline lifts her legs up, she might have gas. Over the past thirty years, Michelle has helped more than fifty babies and their mommas find comfort in the world. Betsy and I, and for that matter Emmeline, would be lost without her. Betsy texts with Michelle nearly every day.

Life requires experts. We need people around us who know what they are doing and can save us from our own mistakes.

In a way this book has been deceptive. It has taught you to become a hero on a mission even though the hero is not the most evolved role. The most aspirational role for any of us is the role of guide.

So why spend so much time teaching people to live as heroes when the goal of life is to become the guide?

The reason is, of course, that we cannot become guides unless we have lived as heroes on a mission.

We have all met hundreds of successful people in dozens of different categories of success. We've met people who are poor but happy, which I would classify as a success. We've met people who are successful in sports, in love, in politics, in science, and in business.

If you look closely at impactful people, you'll notice they vary in their beliefs, their religions, and even their skill sets. It's difficult to find commonalities the rest of us can repeat. Some impactful people are quiet while others are charismatic.

The one characteristic I notice about nearly all of them, though, is that they are competent.

By competence I mean they have been seasoned. They have been through the gauntlet of life and come out smart, wise, and capable. You might even call them tough. By tough I don't mean slow-walking, gun-toting, side-of-mouth-talking Clint Eastwood types. I'd consider Stephen Hawking more tough than Clint Eastwood, and Hawking was none of those things.

When I say tough, I mean they are able to successfully navigate difficult conditions. To be able to navigate difficult conditions without being taken down by them, you have to have experience. Heroes on a mission become guides because they have learned from their hardships and mistakes. Experts are experts because they have been through the fire.

Nassim Nicholas Taleb describes these people as "antifragile." In his book by the same name, Taleb writes about the risk of people becoming weak because of systems that are overstructured or in which people are overcoddled. His point is that we grow and prosper when we are disrupted because disruption forces us to change into stronger versions of ourselves.

To live as a hero on a mission is not about living a life filled with joy and ease. Pause any movie and ask yourself if the hero would rather be in some other situation. The answer will undoubtedly be *yes*. Life is difficult and cannot be fully controlled. And yet every sailor knows that while they cannot control the wind, they can harness it. If the wind is blowing at their backs, they can sail fast; and if the wind is blowing in their face, they can sail slow. But they can always sail.

Viktor Frankl's ideas do not ensure that life will go well for us. They simply ensure that we experience meaning whether or not life goes well. His theories, after all, were crystallized in a concentration camp.

Mental, physical, and spiritual competence happens when we move into the challenges life offers us. Victims do not face these challenges because they cannot. Villains cause many of these challenges. Heroes walk into and through the challenges and are transformed in the process. Guides, then, teach heroes all they know about how to surmount the challenges.

Guides teach us how to have courage because they have lived a life of courage themselves.

The reason we want to live as heroes on a mission is, the more we do so, the sooner we will transform into guides.

It will be tempting for you to think of yourself as a guide too early. Of course we all have guide energy that we can summon, even as children. We can always help somebody else win. But to fully become the guide, we must have lived for years as a hero on a mission, conquering our fears and learning from our tragedies.

Do not trust a person to guide you up Mount Everest if they have never been to the Himalayas.

Deciding where you are going in your life rather than allowing fate to dictate your direction is a characteristic of competence. Knowing the difference between a primary task that must be achieved and a secondary task that should be ignored is a characteristic of competence. Choosing to forgive requires emotional intelligence, which personifies competence. Living in gratitude rather than wallowing in pity is a perspective that demands a control of one's mind, another characteristic of competence.

Competence involves the ability to encounter difficult circumstances and grow from them rather than be destroyed by them. The more we experience life as a hero on a mission, the more we learn and the more we can pass down.

THE CHARACTERISTICS OF A GUIDE

You can tell a good guide by the qualities they bring to the journey. Here are four characteristics I believe are most critical to develop in order to help others.

Experience

One of the reasons guides are often so old in stories is because the writer (and audience) knows they must have experience. Picture Gandalf's white beard or Yoda's limp and cane.

When we talk about experience, what we actually mean is a backstory. Often, the people we most respect have been through what we are going through and survived. Guides teach heroes how they did it, and as such, generational wisdom is passed down.

Haymitch had won the Hunger Games years before Katniss offered herself as tribute. Because of his experience, he was able to help Katniss win the day.

Heroes in stories who see themselves as equals to their guide rub readers the wrong way. Deep within us, we know that respect must be earned, not demanded. We can't skip the wisdom-creating process. We respect a guide who has experience.

There is no reason to rush in our effort to become the guide. We simply need to live as a hero on a mission.

Wisdom

With experience comes wisdom. And the primary source of wisdom is failure.

What's interesting about heroes in stories is that they are not often competent. With the exception of the final few scenes of a story in which they face and defeat the villain, the hero has been a bumbling, fearful mess. A story is more interesting when the hero narrowly gets out of their challenges alive.

Often, stories layer scenes of progress and setback, stacking failures on top of narrow escapes. Why? Partly for suspense but partly because we know a hero is going to have to gain strength in order to meet the villain as an equal. The hero will have to be strong and wise, and the only way to gain strength and wisdom is to fail and then succeed, over and over.

Again, our victim mentality will tempt us to succumb to failures rather than learn from them. Heroes learn, and learning is how they grow and eventually become the guide.

Empathy

Villains and guides are strong. In fact, the villain is often the strongest character in the story, until the end when, hopefully, they are defeated. This is one of the reasons people are drawn to villains. It explains Mussolini and Hitler. People mistake a villain for a guide because of their strength.

But guide strength is different. Guide strength is reined in by altruism. The guide's glory is in their past. Now they are trying to help somebody else achieve glory. Having entered battle themselves, they know the world is at war and want light to defeat darkness. The world, to a guide, is larger than themselves and their personal story. Guides care.

Villain strength invites us to join them in establishing our superiority, control, and power. Guide strength invites us to restore justice, defend true victims, and create equality through opportunity.

To watch Michelle talk to Betsy about our baby is to watch a master encourager. When she instructs Betsy and me on how to comfort and feed the baby, her words are soft and kind, her smile absolutely radiant, and her celebrations of Betsy's victories are fist-clenching, arm-raising expressions of joy. When the baby latches, Michelle dances a jig. When the baby poops, Michelle delightfully announces the process is working!

Guides bring the light to humble heroes who are inexperienced and afraid.

The guide passes down more than wisdom; they pass down compassion and empathy. They have been defeated themselves and have climbed back; they know how it feels to be tempted by helplessness. They have been misunderstood, so they seek to understand. They have been abandoned, so they are loyal.

The best definition I've heard for the word *empathy* is "shared pain."

The guide carries some of the hero's burden, allowing the hero to travel farther and faster.

Sacrifice

Empathy, however, is not enough to seal somebody's identity as the guide. Actual sacrifice is necessary.

In stories, guides give up their wisdom, their time, their money, and at times their lives so the hero can prevail. They do this knowing that their time, wisdom, and money will not buy them glory. They are in it for the hero's glory and to contribute to another victory of light over darkness.

Often, guides make the ultimate sacrifice for the hero. The war between darkness and light is that important to them. Remember, a guide's life is no longer lived for self. A guide sacrifices so that light can defeat darkness.

When Romeo scales the wall into the Capulet courtyard, we see a classic scene in which a guide imparts wisdom to a hero and also a nod to the ultimate sacrifice a guide often commits for a hero.

As Romeo comes under Juliet's window, she is engaging in a discourse with two stars above, symbolizing that she is one-third of a divine trinity. In fact, Romeo describes her as a *winged messenger of heaven*. In the play, she is the strong and competent guide and Romeo is the hero.

Even though she is young, merely thirteen, Shakespeare imparts divine and eternal wisdom to her and offers, through her, a path for Romeo to find resolution and redemption.

In short, Juliet is positioned as the Christ figure in the play.

Later in the scene, the two talk about how their names (natures) keep them apart. Romeo then gives agency to Juliet, asking her to *call me by another name and I'll no longer be a Montague.*

This is biblical imagery, of course. Romeo believes that his union with Juliet will change his nature.

Then, in an effort to fool their parents, Juliet sips a poison that will put her in a death-like sleep. She "dies" then rises from the dead. When she wakes, she learns that Romeo himself had been fooled and had taken his life to be with her. She then takes her own life saying she will go to be with him where there is a wedding in waiting.

I believe Shakespeare made Juliet the Christ figure in the play as an effort to teach a more relational (Protestant) theology to the Catholics who were warring for power in England. Regardless, the precepts of the Christian gospel, just as in many ancient stories, involve a divine guide sacrificing their life for a hero suffering a painful journey toward absolution.

In the Christian Gospels, Jesus Himself is a guide helping heroic sinners find resolution and as such come home where there is a wedding to be performed at a feast in heaven. The guide, then, sacrifices for the troubled and fearful hero in an attempt to help them toward the climactic scene of their absolution.

In Shel Silverstein's beautiful children's book *The Giving Tree*, the tree itself plays the guide, helping the hero child through their life journey, always giving of its apples, then its branches, and finally its trunk until the tree itself lays down the last bit of its life for the child.

Charlotte, the spider in E. B. White's book *Charlotte's Web*, gave up her life to save the life of her friend Wilbur the pig.

These guides gave up their lives to help a hero resolve their story and contribute to light's defeat of darkness.

And these beautiful sacrifices aren't isolated in literature. Only seconds ago in the café where I am typing these words, a woman let her plate and muffin fly so she could grip her child as she fell on a step. It is in our very nature to protect those who come behind us and give up our safety for their glory.

As we surface guide energy, helping others win, we find a deeper and deeper experience of meaning. It is in us all to become guides.

But, of course, this takes time. As Betsy and I nurture the soil in our garden, I recognize that the hero must grow, slowly. Peter's knowledge of trees grew as slowly as the trees themselves. He is passing down a legacy to us that we can pass down to Emmeline.

All those years achieving glory as heroes, while important for training, are hardly the point of life. The point is to become the guide, to demonstrate the inclination of altruism and serve as an example for others.

The less we play the victim and the less we play the villain, the more we find ourselves playing the roles of hero and guide.

Starting with the end in mind, bringing something good into the world, accepting life's challenges, and sharing our lives with others is the path to transformation.

In the end, guides are just heroes who kept going.

15

· · · · · · · · · · · · · ·

The Story Goes On and On

AN OLD FRIEND ONCE told me a story. He was graduating from college and decided to spend a year traveling around the world. In a final meeting before he left, his mentor told him that when he returned he did not want to recognize him.

"Well, I'll be doing a lot of hiking, so I imagine I'll be in great shape," my friend said.

"That's not what I'm talking about," his mentor said. "I mean I want you to become such a better version of yourself that it is as if the old you has been shed like a skin. You'll leave the old you behind as you learn to manage money, discern whom to befriend, manage your body, manage your spirit, learn to rest, and to believe in yourself."

My friend was intimidated by the conversation. Yet, as he traveled around Europe, he looked for opportunities to transform. How would he respond to setbacks? Would he be a loyal friend? Would he take risks, show courage, and navigate a year worth remembering?

In short, he kept asking himself the question, "What would my best self do in this situation?" And with that started to practice becoming a better version of himself.

My friend said he grew more during that year than in any year previous.

The challenge to become unrecognizable is a challenge life hands to each of us, day after day, year after year.

Healthy things grow and change and so do healthy people.

From the day we are born to the day we die, we never stop changing. In every chapter of our lives it is possible to become better and better versions of ourselves.

When we say to ourselves, "I'm not much of an athlete," or "I am super shy in front of groups," we fall into what Carol Dweck calls a fixed mindset. The Stanford professor claims a fixed mindset correlates with lesser wages, worse relationships, and higher levels of anxiety.

Instead, she invites her students into a growth mindset. A growth mindset means we believe we are always changing and can make enormous transformations in our lives. When we have a growth mindset, we believe we can get good at something if we apply ourselves. For instance, instead of saying, "I'm terrible at math," we should say, and think, "I'm not good at math because I've not chosen to apply myself just yet."

In other words, Dweck believes we shouldn't paint ourselves into a corner when it comes to our identity. When we think of ourselves, we should think of ourselves as fluid beings, able to change.

Change, though, requires effort. In order to transform, we have to engage and perhaps even embrace the conflict that comes when we apply ourselves to a vision.

STORIES BEGIN AND END

It wouldn't matter if we transformed if our lives on earth went on forever. But they don't. Our stories have a beginning and middle and end, of course, but they also have something else: a moral.

The stories we live don't affect only us, they affect the people around us. Our stories teach the people around us what is worth living for and what is worth dying for.

About twenty-five years ago, my friend Bruce Deel moved into the most dangerous neighborhood in Atlanta, Georgia. He and his family moved into a church and lived there for years. Bruce and his wife, Rhonda, rescued young women who were being sex trafficked, young men who were caught up in gangs, elderly neighbors who needed medical care, and addicts who felt they were no longer in control of their lives. As he established himself and his family in the neighborhood, they were constantly under threat. They've had multiple cars stolen, found a homeless man living under the baptistry, and Bruce has even been shot at and engaged in knife fights.

I asked him once how he could justify risking his life when he has a wife and children at home. He said leaving a legacy of courage to his children might have to cost him his life and that if he died, he'd die as an example to his family of a man who boldly loved and attempted to help his community.

Today, Bruce and Rhonda still live in the neighborhood. They have a multiacre compound called City of Refuge that is often considered one of the most successful social impact programs in the country. They have a cooking school, a coding academy, a medical clinic, and a safe house for trafficked girls. They take in prisoners when they are let out of prison and train them to do meaningful work.

What we do with our lives matters. And each of us is running out of time.

In the months I've spent writing this book, I've watched stories begin and stories come to an end. Lucy has weeks, not months, to live. She's taking an hour or more in the morning to stand up. She's outlived the average life span of a chocolate Lab by nearly two years. We hide an anti-inflammatory in her food and sit and scratch her head until the pill helps her gain strength. She's comforted by my presence, so I've stopped traveling in order to be around. She watches as Betsy and I go in and out of the nursery. She lifts her nose when she hears the baby cry as though to catch a sniff of the newest member of the family.

It is clear that her story is coming to an end.

There is joy happening too. Emmeline is growing, fast. She smiles, now. You can tickle her. She looks around the room and recognizes people and wiggles until they come over and say hello. In a couple of months she will be crawling, then soon after that walking the trails at Goose Hill. We will watch as she begins her long, natural transformation from victim to hero.

Both the pain and joy of this life are beautiful to me. We will soon bury Lucy under the oak tree in the side yard, the one where Betsy's name and my name are carved inside a heart.

The truth is, we can all go much further in this life than we ever thought. Leaving a victim mentality behind, where it belongs, is like dropping a bag of rocks. We'll move faster, I promise.

Years ago, I was invited to spend time with a prominent American family that had built several multibillion-dollar companies. A few of the family members had read my books and asked me to come to one of their family reunions. The family often invites authors and speakers to their family meetings as a way of facilitating multigenerational conversations. The whole thing was a strategic story dreamed up by the family to prevent the deterioration that almost always happens when families start gaining and managing wealth. I was honored. I found them to be especially humble people and genuinely kind.

One of the most winsome things about the family is that, as they introduced me to one another, they would refer to the different generations as generation one, generation two, and so on. There were four generations present, and one of the young women in generation four was about to birth generation five.

Having grown up in a single-parent home and because my grandfather died before I was born, the whole idea of a multigenerational family, especially one that spans five generations, was all new to me.

Sometimes when I walk around Goose Hill, I wonder what Emmeline will think when she is very old, when her story is nearly done, and she visits this place with her children and grandchildren. I would like to live such a story that she tells her children about her own generation one, about how her mother and father built this place and raised her here and showed her a love story she could imitate. I hope she talks about how much generation one invited artists and thinkers and gardeners and leaders from around the world to think and dream and create. I wonder if she will know we did it mostly for her, so she could grow up around people who dream and then make dreams happen.

You and I may or may not come from a powerful or positive legacy, but every single one of us gets to leave one.

I can't control how Emmeline perceives me. That's her business. But I can give her love, security, and an example to follow. My story can positively affect her story. The decision to do so is not up to fate. It is up to me.

When we live a life of meaning, we invite others to do the same. Those who come behind us will build on our stories. They can add to them and make them better because we have showed them the way.

Life can be very difficult, I know. There are tragedies all around us. There is darkness. But don't forget, there is also light. We get to participate in the making of that light.

When the existential vacuum comes for you, and it will, remember there is a hope that is very real in the world.

We can always make meaning.

ACT
3

Your Life Plan and Daily Planner

We've included space to create your life plan in this section of the book. You can write your eulogy, your ten-year, five-year, and one-year visions, and your goals. There are even a few days of the HOAM Daily Planner.

If you want to continue to use the planner and life plan, you can download these pages for free and print off as many copies of them as you like. Just visit HeroOnAMission.com or use the QR code at the beginning of this book.

If you enjoy helping people find their mission and experience a deep sense of meaning, apply to be a HOAM facilitator at HeroOnAMission.com.

My Eulogy

My Life Plan Ten-Year Vision

If a movie was made about your life this year, what would it be called?

_____

Age

_____

Career

- _____
- _____
- _____

Health

- _____
- _____
- _____

Family

- _____
- _____
- _____

Friends

- _____
- _____
- _____

Spiritual

- _____
- _____

- _____
- _____

2 things I try to do every day

- _____
- _____

2 things I don't do

- _____
- _____

The central theme of my story at this point is

_____

My Life Plan Five-Year Vision

If a movie was made about your life this year, what would it be called?

_____

Age

_____

Career

- _____
- _____
- _____

Health

- _____
- _____
- _____

Family

- _____
- _____
- _____

Friends

- _____
- _____
- _____

Spiritual

- _____
- _____

- _____
- _____

2 things I try to do every day

- _____
- _____

2 things I don't do

- _____
- _____

The central theme of my story at this point is

_____

My Life Plan One-Year Vision

If a movie was made about your life this year, what would it be called?

_____

Age

_____

Career

- _____
- _____
- _____

Health

- _____
- _____
- _____

Family

- _____
- _____
- _____

Friends

- _____
- _____
- _____

Spiritual

- _____
- _____

- _____
- _____

2 things I try to do every day

- _____
- _____

2 things I don't do

- _____
- _____

The central theme of my story at this point is

_____

Goal name

Why does this goal matter to you?

Completion date

Goal partners

Milestones

1.
2.
3.

Daily sacrifices

Repetition record

Goal name

Why does this goal matter to you?

Completion date

Goal partners

Milestones

1
2
3

Daily sacrifices

Repetition record

Goal name

Why does this goal matter to you?

Completion date

Goal partners

Milestones
1
2
3

Daily sacrifices

Repetition record

Hero on a Mission Daily Planner

Date _____

☐ I've read my eulogy   ☐ I've reviewed my vision worksheets   ☐ I've reviewed my goals

Primary task one

_____
_____
_____
_____

If you could live this day again, what would you do differently this time?

• _____
• _____
• _____

Primary task two

_____
_____
_____
_____

What am I grateful for today?

• _____
• _____
• _____
• _____

Appointments

• _____
• _____
• _____
• _____
• _____

Secondary tasks

☐ _____   ☐ _____
☐ _____   ☐ _____
☐ _____   ☐ _____
☐ _____   ☐ _____

Hero on a Mission Daily Planner

Date _____

☐ I've read my eulogy ☐ I've reviewed my vision worksheets ☐ I've reviewed my goals

Primary task one
_____
_____
_____
_____
_____

If you could live this day again, what would you do differently this time?
- _____
- _____
- _____

Primary task two
_____
_____
_____
_____
_____

What am I grateful for today?
- _____
- _____
- _____
- _____

Appointments
- _____
- _____
- _____
- _____
- _____

Secondary tasks
☐ _____ ☐ _____
☐ _____ ☐ _____
☐ _____ ☐ _____
☐ _____ ☐ _____

Hero on a Mission Daily Planner

Date

☐ I've read my eulogy ☐ I've reviewed my vision worksheets ☐ I've reviewed my goals

Primary task one
_____
_____
_____
_____
_____

If you could live this day again, what would you do differently this time?
· _____
· _____
· _____

Primary task two
_____
_____
_____
_____
_____

What am I grateful for today?
· _____
· _____
· _____
· _____

Appointments
· _____
· _____
· _____
· _____
· _____

Secondary tasks
☐ _____ ☐ _____
☐ _____ ☐ _____
☐ _____ ☐ _____
☐ _____ ☐ _____

Index

. . . .

About the Author

· ·

Donald Miller is the CEO of *Business Made Simple* and the author of ten books, including *Building a StoryBrand* and *Blue Like Jazz*. He and his wife Betsy along with their daughter Emmeline live in Nashville, Tennessee.

This book comes with a free Hero on a Mission Life Plan and Daily Planner. Scan the QR code below to download your life plan and daily planner pages: